Published in the United States by SECOPE Inc.

ISBN: 9781798509524

10987 65432

IN LOVE WE STILL TRUST

LESSONS WE LEARNED FROM MARTIN LUTHER KING JR., AND SR.

DR. VIRGIL A. WOOD

WITH A FORWARD BY WYATT TEE WALKER

For my beloved wife Lillian who, for more than sixty-five years, has been a major conduit of divine love into my life in every way conceivable.

Thank you again, Dr. Wyatt Tee Walker, who reminded me: "You should have said these are lessons we all learned from King."

Still learning, I'm now at work on my next move, *Reconciliation Jubilee.*

Presented to _____

On _____

By _____

On the Occasion of _____

_____

_____

_____

Table of Contents

Foreword by
Dr. Wyatt "Tee" Walker

If l may say so, I really enjoyed your book, In Love We Trust. I found it very analytical. You have done more to talk about what King taught us than anybody I've read, and I have read almost everything there is about King.

Your book is more substantive about his make up than anything that I've seen. Most books talk about what he did, but you have delved into his personhood. And I think that's what makes your book unique.

Secondly, I want to thank you for your analysis of Malcolm X. I appreciated that more than anything I've seen, and your analysis of Rosa Parks lets me know her in a way that I never knew her before. And I think that's very meaningful for people who know her name, but who do not know her. And for those of us who know her, we never got a chance to know her as you have analyzed her, against the background of the enneagramd and your ttz t®. It helps the reader to understand the relationships and the persons you are describing.

You have also approached the Beloved Community in a different way; you know, it was something spiritual to us, generally. But you have delved into the economics of the Beloved Community, which is more sound and more biblical than any of us ever believed,---well, certainly, myself included. But, it will make a real contribution to our literature if people read and take seriously what you have done and analyzed.

I was astounded when I read about your Reversing the Jail Trail Project, and how you and Dr. Owen Cardwell, and one of my Doctoral Students, Dr. James Coleman, went to see Dr. Jerry Falwell to get his involvement in reversing and shutting off the Jail Trail in our communities and nation, and the Summit that followed. That's very important, and the Jubilee Project for

Reversing the Jail Trail is another concept that is original with you, and it is important to our young men.

Ophrah Winfrey said the other day, "If you want to see more good looking Black and Hispanic men, go to the jail. And they are really smart." She was right because I've been to many jails and prisons, and the Black and Hispanic young men of marriageable age are incarcerated.

This work can help them find, enjoy, and be led where their potential can take them.

-Dr. Wyatt "Tee" Walker, celebrated chief of staff for MLK and his SCLC during its formative years

Chester, Virginia
July 2005

Acknowledgments

How does one accurately acknowledge and thank all those who have been directly responsible for bringing forth this work, In Love We Trust?

I do so with humility and gratitude, for all the indispensable help I have received along the way, and with fear and trepidation at the thought of possibly leaving out one single person whose direct help was instrumental in this undertaking.

First, Uncle Jesse, grandfather to my maternal cousins, Grandma Callie, Rosa L. Parks, H. W. B. Walker, Sue Ridley Williams, Mary Carr Greer, Chelsea Clark, Henry J. McGuinn, Samuel D. Proctor, Herbert Gezork, John Scammon, Daddy King, Derald Langham, Robert Greenleaf, David McClelland, Chris Argyris, Ken Haskins, Manny Zimmerman, Harvey Cox, Benjamin E. Mays, Leon H. Sullivan, Gus Roman, L. D. Reddick, Cleveland Chandler, Frank Davis, Walter Little, Henry Fields, L. Francis Griffin, John Young, William Baker, Bates Ford, Benjamin H. Wright, H. Naylor Fitzhugh, Steve Kane, whose continbution was early in this effort, Louis O. Kelso, Don Richard Riso, Russ Hudson, Macy Reid, Kathy Hurley, Theodore Donson, Owen Cardwell, Paul Chapman, Earl Lawson, John Harmon, James Breeden, Theodore Burton, Norman Kurland, Walter Fauntroy, Freeman A. Hrabowski III; Fields Wood, Robert Winfrey, H.Q. Thompson, Melvin Penn, MD, Judy Sedgeman, Sydney Banks, Willian Pettit, MD, Deborah Prothrow-Stith, Md, Roger Mills, Father Peter Young, Russell Quaglia, and Jack Pransky, both of whom the Author collaborated closely with in designing Chater Four. And finally my own family-a highly interactive and love-committed community: David, Deborah, Lorene. And with special acknowledgement of your potential for greatness, grandsons Christopher and Jordan, and all the children and youth of the nations and of the congregations and communities I have had the privilege to serve, with much love and thanks to every one of you. And finally, to Lillian, I acknowl-edge and honor your great gifts of love which have been mine, not only in the writing of this book, but for 65-plus years as my wife and sweetheart.

Introduction

This book is written and addressed to my brothers and sisters of the Jubilee black church; to the extended African-American community; to the white church—Protestant, Roman Catholic, and Orthodox—and to the American community as a whole ... extending a warm invitation for eavesdropping to our brothers and sisters of the broader world, Jewish and Muslim, especially in Africa and Jerusalem—and with other historic faith communities as well.

This book is written to the whole Christian family of the world, and indeed, to the whole human family. It is a book about Christian heroes and heroines—initially Afro-Christian men and women—who fully engaged the forces and resources of their time on behalf of Christ, their African race, and the whole human race.

First, to the black church, because of all institutions today, it is widely acknowledged as the most promising for bringing together the black race in a rare combination of coalitions, dedicated to lifting and climbing together, and for eliminating dependency and poverty from its ranks. As the black church goes, so goes the race, for better or worse.

Second, it is important for the black church to know that it must be the major servant-leader institution to synergize the total salvation—economic, social, political, and spiritual—of the African-American community here and abroad. Likewise, it is important for the African-American community itself to know that its total salvation comes by working with, embracing, and supporting that common bridge over which we must all walk. It cannot ignore the black church and, at the same time, depend on it for help, for we must become willing and loving partners. The same holds true for church, town, and gown, if this healing of the soul of black America is to take place, as well as the healing of the soul of all America.

Finally, the white church must follow—not lead—the black church in the matters being set forth here. Those from the white church who already know this are our real allies and partners in the total salvation of our race. Others who pretend this are simply extending old patterns of dominance, with a new smiling face.

This book started in the heart of a little boy who listened to his grandmother pray at the dinner table. She always closed her prayer with the words of psalm writer, King David, "I have been young, and now am old, yet have I not seen the righteous forsaken, nor his seed begging bread" (Psalm 37:25, King James Version). Something within me connected with her prayers, making my soul say "yes."

My maternal grandma, Callie Brown, had a remarkable sense of calm that matched the economy of sufficiency that my mother and father, Marion and Frances Wood, provided for their family. They operated from that sense of trust in God, which enabled them to do whatever things honorable they and our neighbors had to do, to make for our families an economy of sufficiency and abundance under the most adverse conditions coming out of the depression.

I knew then as a seven-year-old boy (1938) what so many others like us knew: that God's economy was not one of scarcity, but one of abundance. My eventual journey through Harvard University in 1973-a furlough from the civil rights movement-to pursue a doctorate in education, confirmed in my head, heart, and soul-now some 35 years later-how that economy of sufficiency and abundance could work for African Americans and all people.

It further confirmed that grandma Callie was correct, although classical economists and creeds postulate economics as really being about scarcity, rather than sufficiency and abundance.

My work with Martin Luther King from 1959 to 1968; meeting and working with Louis Kelso, binary economist and great humanitarian; and bringing King and Kelso together in 1967 to discuss the forthcoming Poor People's Campaign led me to see the real truth.

That truth was how we could create the beloved economy of character, cash, and culture, by developing the plan, the will, and the operation to see it through.

A second critical truth with which we must begin (and on which we must build) is that none of this can be accomplished until the groundwork for authentic "peoplehood" is established. Authentic peoplehood begins with the process of naming ourselves in a spiritually correct way.

Nobody knows our name ... we don't know our own name. Our name in this book will be "Amafrican." Wherever one lives within the diaspora, it will feel right to speak of ourselves as Amafrican.

Here's one more effort by an African American to determine our own name. We ourselves, the black descendants of mother Africa in the diaspora, must settle this once and for all—if we can. A day does not pass, when the mainstream media does not insult this great and proud people, adding to our general shame and depression. To write our proud name in lowercase is an insult that must end now. Every time, we are referred to by a name that is grammatically correct, but spiritually wrong: "blacks," "minorities" ... we must make the effort towards spiritual correctness.

The result of my own research (and conversations with persons on both sides of the continent about the matter) suggests that it would be most advantageous for us to refer to ourselves as Amafrican, in the same spirit as the reference to the American born of Asian descent is called "Amerasian." Our reference to ourselves as Amafrican never fails to elicit a joyful rightness and delight in every person with whom I have raised it.

Hence, the reference in this book to African Americans will be noted as Amafrican, as it is consistent with the context. Couldn't we just try it on for size, then evaluate? This effort would simply be part of our effort to find out who we really are.

In his book, Black Theology and Youths at Risk, David Mitchell helps us understand the steps we must take to discover who we are. It begins with self-examination; it then progresses from self-dissatisfaction to self-evaluation; and finally, self-realization of our identity and potential as a people of the whole, contributing to the nation of the whole.

This may be a flawed and partial book, as most (even good books) are ... how like humanity. However, I pray and trust that it is a truthful book, and that it will be useful, leading Americans and world citizens to discuss and debate its salient issues.

Let the soul of America be moved definitively beyond denial towards healing. Then we will have laid the sure foundation for freedom and happiness over despair and want, for all American citizens.

A twelve-step national dialogue, at the kitchen table of every home seeking to dive into the joy and depth of its own soul, is a sure and certain way ahead. Such a move will be a re-confirmation and recommitment to the spiritual (yet flawed) roots our founding fathers intended Americans to build upon. And build we must, or come apart at the seams.

The mounting evidence is all around. Those with eyes to see will see. Many can already see a new America, choosing the high road of healing, a restored American soul becoming the real treasure unto which the nations of the earth can aspire. America can become a great mentor nation for the many that need a better model than they now have. The nation with a beloved economy will be the crown jewel among the true wonders of the world. This is my story—my dream for the new America, and the beloved world community.

For me, all this is premised upon the probability that when the historic faith communities who share the spiritual legacy of Abraham, Jewish, Christian, and Islamic—hear, ponder, and discuss the words found in II Chronicles 7:14, they will confirm that the bedrock spirituality of our faith mandates soul healing.

"If my people, who are called by my name (i.e. Jubilee People), will humble themselves and pray and seek my face and turn from their wicked ways, then will I hear from heaven and will forgive their sin and will heal their land." (New International Version)

"If my own people will humbly pray and turn back to me and stop sinning, then will I answer them from heaven, I will forgive them, and make their land fertile once again." (Contemporary English Version)

The greatest lesson I learned from Martin Luther King was how to trust love. As persons committed to living and sharing the good life, living the Beloved Community, as King styled it—we must stand ever vigilant at the gate of truth, rediscover and apply the truth enshrined on our money, In God We Trust. King's faith tells us that to trust love, is to trust in God. Our challenge is to make it real. Finding and sharing this truth, as King's life and works make clear, can lead the world beyond chaos to community, the Beloved Community.

Our founding fathers and brothers seemed ready for something far more profound when they laid the foundations of this new republic, our America. They seemed to sense that we were called to greatness, when we were not yet even good. They laid that foundation so that later generations would find the right words to match our search. When they did, they coined it in the words of the Apostle John's New Testament letter: "In God (who is love) we trust."

It would take a son of the enslaved Africa people of America—Martin Luther King, Jr—to speak the word of truth, with love, to a powerful America. As a teacher would a classroom of kindergartners, he taught us to say it—haltingly at first: "In love we trust."

Now comes King's disciple and friend, lifting up his clear and compelling words, along with the wisdom we garnered, gleanings since King last physically spoke to us. I come to challenge us all to learn and live by the principle of trusting God and love. If we—as that vast part of the nation that affirms beloved America over ugly America—are willing and will hold a sustained dialogue with one another in places private as well as public, we will find compelling reasons to leave un-tampered, "In God we trust."

Since the whole earth has been called to greatness, and now that America for all has at least and at last become good, we-as the people of the whole nation-have the potential to become great by recalling and reclaiming King's prescient prescriptions for a Beloved Community in our own time, space and place.

What must now happen is that Beloved America and ugly America must get on speaking terms with each other, and engage themselves in an honest rediscovery of soul as set forth by King, with all its faith communities focusing their dialogue around a central question: How does my particular faith (Christianity, Judaism, Islam, and others), soulfully add to King's conversation around the intersection of love and community, giving us the possibility of living the Beloved Community?

Such a dialogue will include King's notions about character, culture, and commerce as the basis for understanding the Beloved Community strivings. However, first must come the understanding and the wisdom upon which new passion feeds, and upon which nobler behavior rests.

This would indeed really be something for Martin. His voice resounds today as eloquently as ever. As he spoke to the nation's conscience, his dream sustained him. It continues to sustain us. From the call for equity to the reality of commerce, "I Have a Dream" is the message of yesterday reverberating throughout today and into tomorrow. As we continue to celebrate his life, now some thirty-five years since his death, we honor his dream with the foundations of a new opportunity for character, culture, and commerce, a place with the recursive effect of his voice, indeed an "EccoPlace" of the soul.

King spoke it in the presence of us all, with that vision of an American Beloved Community, giving us as his legatees the major opportunity to invite that love to infuse our every community, and thus achieve the higher consciousness which energizes ordinary into beloved communities, everywhere.

With a one-year, intensive dialogue throughout our land, (we might call it the National Kitchen Table Summit) I believe we would yield such an abundance of healing, peace, and prosperity that it would surprise and delight us all. It could be launched on January 15 of one year and concluded on January 15 of the next. No one wants less. Everyone wants more.

One symptom of our malaise is educational systems all over America—the sending of black and Hispanic males to prison rather than to university—is the result of education without soul. A nation fostering education without soul is a nation on the way to its own doom. King gave us the formula any nation can use for building soul into its major institutions so that they are based on organized love-mindedness.

In that new spirit, about 10 years ago—after I overcame my lingering resentment of the land that had so mistreated my ancestors and their offspring and learned the basis for being passionately in love with beloved America—I was able to sing again, "My Country 'tis of Thee," as well as "America the Beautiful." I even discovered that I could now pray for and with both Americas with equal passion. Capable of accepting both tracks, I found the wisdom and the words to pray for both in the same room.

Thus, on Thursday, June 12, 2003, upon the kind invitation of Senators Jack Reed and Lincoln Chaffee of my adopted beloved state of Rhode Island, I was able to stand in the well of the United States Senate, and open up my soul in prayer. As we move in greater numbers and with deeper depths into this National Kitchen Table Summit, with the challenge of making the promise and potential of America more real for all its people, we will indeed know more, feel greater, and do better, for Self, Others, Nature, and God. What a SONG, Grandma's song, we can all then sing together! Yes, we could then celebrate whatever early signs and hints of love in Beloved America we uncover up front, as we follow that new spirit leading us all forward and beyond.

Those who embrace this possibility are invited to reflect on this, The June 12th Prayer.

Dear God,

We thank you for the remnants of love that remain within beloved America.

We confess that far too often, we have embraced the anti-love, in thought, word, and deed. Please forgive us, and mend our every flaw.

In the conflicts of life itself, may we find the courage to meditate, to ponder, and to wrestle with the principalities and the powers.

When the conscious light of your love breaks through our common journey, may we take off our shoes and worship, for that indeed will have become holy ground.

Grant us grace, dear God, to go forward and match deeds of love to our sacred words, that the love-which is in the community of all humanity-may perfect itself in us.

Having come now to understand how we of all faiths, races, and nationalities-as one people under God-could go forward, may we forever trust and abide in love.

And in the name of the one God of love, we offer this prayer. Amen

As a prescription for the healing of the soul of America, it is also necessary and good, for all the nations of the earth.

God bless America and all nations, as they seek this healing of the soul and to be thankful as it unfolds. God help and heal ugly America. God bless beloved America. And yes, beloved America, whatever others do, you bless God!

Shall we get started?

Part One: Faith Beyond Doubt

"Can these bones live?" Ezekiel 37:3a

Chapter 1

My Journey to the Beloved Community

From the family chicken coop-by way of a hometown oak tree—
to Harvard, and beyond ...

My journey to the Beloved Community has been a lifelong trip. When I got there-as Dr. King, had predicted we all would-after my fifty years of involvement in the work, I saw and experienced things that I thought would never come to pass in this life.

In a way, it started on a bright spring morning in 1938, when my father, Marion J. Wood, Sr., took his younger son of seven years into the chicken house, and gave him his first assignment of family responsibility.

I was responsible for feeding and giving water to 150 chickens, keeping the henhouse clean, and gathering the eggs at the end of the day. These tasks would have to be done early, before the two-room schoolhouse just up the road opened for classes; then later, after school; and before a welcome snack and the mandatory homework.

Little did I know then that I was being inducted into a family ritual ofresponsibility, which would lead me unerringly over time, towards my grandfather Alexander's jubilee cosmology, and ultimately, to the origination of SoulScope®.

It would prove to be a very satisfying journey, and the chicken house assignment would become only second in importance to what my father and beloved mother, Frances Brown Wood, made available to me. The most exciting and important lesson would turn out to be the careful path by which they led me to Christ in the home church, which was just across the street from the two-room schoolhouse. This lesson took place a few years after the chicken coop assignment, during the World War II years, under the pastorate of Dr. H.W.B. Walker, an extraordinary shepherd of our flock. I am now certain that these landmark events led me to the town oak tree in the backyard of Mr. Jesse Jackson, Sr., at the age of seventeen. Tall and erect, in spite of 95 years of struggle and labor, Mr. Jackson was 10 years old when the slaves were set free. Now almost blind, he met me dutifully at 7:00 a.m. He sat on the hardwood stool he carved, and with his unlit corncob pipe in and out of his mouth, gave me information about the heritage and history of our little rural community, the elegance and authenticity of which is unrivaled, despite many years of formal study and learning in many high places of academia.

It was at this time in 1948, that I first heard about the biblical jubilee, and how our enslaved ancestors embraced it as the ultimate symbol of their freedom. It would be another twelve years-long after Virginia Union University (1952), and Andover Newton Theological School (1956)-before the jubilee trail would pick up for me: when I joined the work of King and his SCLC. But even then, it would be still another twelve years before reflection and serious study at Harvard University afforded me the understanding of what I believed God had really been doing in the lives of our fathers and mothers, and that of all our awesome ancestors, and Dr. King, and ours.

In time, I would come to really understand that in order to have full appreciation for the universal significance of King's work, one would have to have some pretty good idea about his "soul print" and "soul work," and how he navigated his spiritual journey, and of the ancestors on whose shoulders King stood, educationally, spiritually, and materially. The SoulScope® is the result of that ten-year, intensive, and focused search.

The search is premised on ten assumptions, which have emerged out of my journey and study of (and with) King, Gandhi, the science of organizational development at Harvard, my engagement with the Enneagram through studies with the eminent Enneagram teachers-Don Richard Riso, Russ Hudson, Kathy Hurley, Ted Donson, and Mary Mortz—to whom I am eternally indebted.

It was at the end of the first week of training with Riso that I became fully convinced that his work was the hands and feet to the general concept of King's notion of the Beloved Community.

To embrace the general idea of a Beloved Community is a great start, but it is only a start. It is much like the findings of our jubilee bible teams, interviewing inner-city youth across America and in South Africa about what they would find useful in a jubilee bible study movement. Their responses were synonymous: "Yes, we appreciate the older generation wanting to bring God's Word to us. Yes, we do want to know what is right. But, what we really want you to do is not just to tell us what it is, but to show us how to do what is right." While the Enneagram and the subsequent SoulScope®- cannot show one how to do what's right, it can provide a cognitive map for the needed journey.

The SoulScope® originated out of these studies, but would not likely have seen the light of day without the background through which I was led (and am now convinced God has been leading me) for the seven decades of my life. My greatest challenge and joy is to make available to the youth of America the path by which they can journey into the region of their own true greatness and joy, avoiding the world of drugs and every distraction, and to find peace and joy that do indeed surpass anything else that we can encounter in this life.

The SoulScope® is a totally new configuration, born out of necessity and urgency, inherent in the crises and stresses of our time. The following ten propositions will sketch out its broad parameters, as a new tool for the 21st century, to help individuals assess and plan their lives, so as to ensure and assure significance and success. It is offered as a guide to an individual's spiritual DNA, with the hope that people will learn how to understand themselves and each other, and get along better.

The ten assumptions that serve as the premise for the SoulScope® will no doubt change, as the result of the dialogue and conversation its usage will engender. At this point, they are as follows:

1. This is a story (your story and mine) that begins with a singing God.

It states that at the conception of every human soul, God sings a doxology. Why is God so excited at the conception of every human?At that point, even mommy and daddy are unaware that conception occurred. But God knows, and God sings. The same God who declared every aspect of creation "good," also classifies procreation as "very good." God probably said "wow" when each of us was conceived!

2. The SoulScope® is the true birthright of every human born into the world. By it, the course for all life will be set-pre-engineered, but not constructed. Success for the SoulScope® aware person, does not focus so much in being dealt a great hand at birth, as it does be in the learning how to play very well, whatever hand life deals you. The dealer is the Creator; parents, family, village and community-both local and national-serve as part of the construction crew.

3. Your SoulScope® marks your highest potential for greatness, achievement, service, immortality, and union with God. It will be a matter of maximizing "heart, mind, body, soul, and strength" around love. People don't naturally know how to do so. Some will refer to this personal attribute as their "divine endowment," one's "spirit fruit" (fruit of the spirit), their "virtue realized," their "spot of grace received and appropriated."

4. Your SoulScope® also marks your most lowdown possibilities; your shadow side; your reigning compulsions; the sin that is original with, and unique to you; your evil spirit-in-waiting. It is living more out of fear than love, sometimes called your root sin. It is the evil spirit that captures your heart, mind, body, and soul in the absence of your commitment to love and decisiveness about "living in the spirit." All the historic faith communities identified their great men and women (sometimes even youth) who made the decision to live by the spirit, and who do in fact make the valiant effort. Jesus said at twelve years of age, "Did you not know that I must [now] be

about my Father's business?"

The Bar Mitzvah, Bas Mitzvah, and other rites of passage, are saying a similar thing. The evil spirit, waiting in hiding, masks the compulsive side of human beings. People who neglect the spirit dimension of their own individual lives never make friends with their dark side. In fact, they deny it and become debilitated by it, pushing it off onto someone else, and thus, projecting and being swayed by it all the more, than if they acknowledged it, dealt with it, tamed it, and then used it creatively, as the dark with their light.

5. All real knowledge (including self-knowledge) begins with learning and knowing ones' own SoulScope®. In time, all education that ultimately neglects knowledge of the learner's true identity, destiny, and pathway to that greatness, fails.

6. Knowledge of your SoulScope® prepares you to avoid costly and irreversible mistakes, which you may spend a lifetime regretting. This includes getting off drugs, or never being hooked in the first place: undrugging the former, and drug-proofing the latter. The claim here is that knowledge and practice of ones' SoulScope® brings about a different kind of intoxication-a high on soul. The applications are as numerous as our painful human predicaments and problems.

Without knowledge of that SoulScope®, we're almost bound to make these irreversible mistakes, which could have been avoided only with this kind of self-knowledge that very few people have at this time.

7. Knowledge of your SoulScope® significantly shortens the learning curve to achievement, success, and deep satisfaction. This applies all across the board, to every level, phase, and type of learning: public, private, secular, religious, formal, or informal. Why should it be necessary to wait until you are on the back end of life to learn the vital lessons that will ensure the success of your life's mission?

If you were blessed with membership in a Beloved Community family (which could compensate for an inadequate nuclear family), where this kind of learning and knowing should be commonplace, you could have learned these lessons on the front end. Sadly, without knowledge of their Soul-Scope®, most people will never really know their unique, God-given, and God-endowed "self" private, secular, religious, formal, or informal. Why should it be necessary to wait until you are on the back end of life to learn the vital lessons that will ensure the success of your life's mission?

If you were blessed with membership in a Beloved Community family (which could compensate for an inadequate nuclear family), where this kind of learning and knowing should be commonplace, you could have learned these lessons on the front end. Sadly, without knowledge of their SoulScope®, most people will never really know their unique, God-given, and God-endowed "self"

8. The SoulScope® can be a major tool for building character empowerment in individuals. This must be the major mission of schools, churches, synagogues, mosques, community organizations, families (especially parents), pastors, priests, imams, teachers, and neighbors and friends, who can offer this tool as a gift because they themselves have already been so blessed.

9. The SoulScope® collectivized is available as one of God's tool for building a kingdom (or community) of character. From this community will flow like-minded culture, commerce, and civilization. It will indeed be Martin Luther King's kind of Beloved Community (global family), of Jews, Christians, Muslims, and all other religions, cultures, nations, tribes, kindred, and even clan, across the face of the entire globe ... wherever the sun runs, and the Internet reaches. Wouldn't it be awesome if humans knew themselves, and then knew each other in terms of our character dimensions, beyond the externalities of life, such as color, as King said we would? It would be a measure of the mind, heart, and soul, not just our physicality.

10. It is the will of the God of love that all our global brothers and sisters be and become all that divinity saw in their SoulScope® on the day when he or she was conceived. SoulScope® gives them access to this mystery for building up their own lives and that of the community.

This mystery of human transformation, renewal, and revitalization will become clearer as the SoulScope® is engaged and used by persons who have decided to engage in a soul search for their own identity, as to who they uniquely are, and where they are (with respect to universal balance or imbalance), and why they are here on Mother Earth, according to divine purpose.

It is our intent to take the SoulScope® into the service of undoping and purpose proofing the youth of this nation and the world, beyond every fear of failure, or any other type. It will afford all youth—especially those who live in at-risk, toxic environments—an internal setup for fulfillment and productivity.

There are many other very exciting applications by which this world and its people can become so much better. Every sane person wants to be more and to do better. That is what it did for me. What God's done for others, God can do for anyone who desires to be more and to do better. Every person can be better at whatever is their own faith community and commitment. Who is to say what the Creator can't do through those who truly do believe, in self, others, nature, and Him?

How to take the Soul Scope® TM Profiler

Go to our website SoulScope.com and review the material there. Then proceed to www.enneagraminstitute.com/rheti, take the enneagram profiler, RHEI, available for a small fee to the Enneagram Institute, whose model originally inspired the Soulscope®. Having determined your number, return to Soulscope®, and discover the journey your spiritual DNA.

Chapter 2

Jubilee Ancestry: Forerunners of the Beloved Community

Dynamic Afro-Christian ancestors who laid the cornerstone for our Beloved Community.

1. **Mary McLeod Bethune** - born in 1875 within the shadow of American slavery, rose to promise as a Christian leader, educator, builder, and advisor to presidents, founder of the National Council of Negro Women, and one of the major mentors of Benjamin Elijah Mays. Her legacy of love is our mandate. Mary McLeod Bethune, born just ten years after slavery ended, rose to become one of the most powerful leaders in America. A collaborator with Roosevelt of the New Deal, her role has been virtually underplayed as a presidential confidant, advisor, and friend. A central part of our story is to gain some understanding of how this woman from such lowly background could rise so high against such odds and take her people by the masses along with her.

2. **Benjamin Elijah Mays** - born in the shadow of Plessy vs. Ferguson in 1896, rose to become a Christian leader, clergyman, educator, America's greatest school master (Lerone Bennett), undisputed mentor to King, and a host of servant leaders. His legacy of excellence and bold leadership is our guide.

If Mary McLeod Bethune can be thought of as the person who got the African American, as well as the American "common man" (as FDR would refer to America's poor and working people), firmly fixed at first base, then it was Mays who got us to second base. Mays was the architect of the new black church, as well as a significant player in the birth of the World Council of Churches and the United Nations. He paved the way for the kind of black church maturity that was absent at the time King was born. By the mid fifties, when King was ready to call into existence a new kind of American body—led by the ecumenical Afro-Christian church, and host to every conceivable sector of good will and productivity in the nation at that time (Protestant, Catholic, Jewish, labor, university, fraternal, civic, and corporate) under the banner of the Southern Christian Leadership Conference—the black church blossomed.

More often credited is his role as King's chief spiritual mentor and close friend, Mays drew great strength and direction from Bethune, founder of what she would later call "the college built on prayer," which she would one day make into a major educational institution: the Bethune Cookman College, of Daytona Beach, Florida.

3. **Martin Luther King, Jr**. -America's apostle of peace and justice; founder of the Southern Christian Leadership Conference; pastor to the globe; Nobel Peace Prize recipient; a modem co-founder of the Beloved Community; a bulwark for the ages; synergy for a new interfaith movement in the world ... his legacy, a Beloved Community, is our challenge.

4. **Samuel Dewitt Proctor** - born in the decade following the First World War, he rose to become great family builder, Christian leader, university president, clergyman, theologian, a founder of the Peace Corps, pastor, educator, and constant source of wisdom and insight for King. He was indeed King's younger mentor (and to hundreds of others) with hands-on involvement. We will not rest 'till we have done the work he bequeathed us. His national youth academy beckons.

5. **James Melvin Washington** - born in 1948 (the season of Gandhi's passing), in the shadow of Tennessee's Lookout Mountains, he rose to

become a distinguished theologian and teacher, awesome author, Christian spokesman, and bridge-builder between the coming and going generations. Taken from us on the short side of his jubilee (two years before his fiftieth birthday), he had so much more to give. We must be true to our conversations with God, and do all in our power to join his work to "reverse soul murder," an important part of his legacy to us.

6. **Fannie Lou Hamer** - born to "too much hard work and too little breathing space," decided to banish "tired of being tired" and almost single-handedly transformed the sweltering political heat of Mississippi and the Democratic Party, into an open door to political participation for "one man/one-woman vote" participation for all Americans. Her efforts at proportional participation in the political process should not be put off ever again.

7. **Valerie E. Russell** - prominent Christian laywoman; head of the Office of Church in Society and of the United Church of Christ; fighter for justice and peace; child of the fifties and sixties, expended her last ounce of life fighting for the causes that she embraced and that captured her. Taken from us at age 55—just five years beyond her jubilee—she already accomplished two lifetimes worth of work. She was mentored by Dr. Dorothy Height, a true legend in her own time. Dr. Height was mentored by Bethune and became her able successor in the National Council of Negro Women in the life of the nation, and the world. The challenges of the open society and of inter-faith cooperation remain hallmarks of Valerie Russell's legacy, the mission that calls us loud and clear.

8. **Sister Thea Bowman** - singer, dancer, liturgist, educator, evangelist—all these roles were embodied in one exuberant woman who was able to find the common thread interweaving people of all races, colors, and creeds. She spent her life preaching the good news as a woman, a black

American, and a Franciscan sister. Another daughter of Mississippi, born December 29, 1937, she fought the good fight against cancer, and just before her death on March 30, 1990, stated: "I've always prayed for the grace to live until I die." (Black Women in America, Carlson Publishing Co., New York: 1993, pg. 155). Her inspiring story will continue to lift the souls of generations who watch her movie and read her books.

9. **Mac Charles Jones** - prominent black Christian leader, pastor, and teacher, he was taken from us just a few years before his jubilee (the fiftieth year). Deputy general secretary of the National Council of Churches of Christ, Howard Thurman scholar and fellow, he spent his latter years reversing the story of "burned down churches being rebuilt," as a result of his great work and vision. His challenge to us is to be globally relevant and locally faithful.

10. **H. Naylor Fitzhugh** - Christian leader, outstanding lay leader, and Sunday school teacher; born about the time when Dubois declared that the problem of his century would be "the problem of the color line," he was a relentless fighter against every kind of injustice. He was the first African-American graduate of the Harvard University Business School, founder of the Howard University Business School, corporate leader, and a founder of AOIP-Assault on Illiteracy Process (also known as Community Motivators), and mentor to generations of corporate and business leaders. Role model of cooperation in church, town and gown, his domain was our blessing.

You must name your own stars, including relatives and your extended family, such as your church, village, town, or gown. The man or woman of all seasons traverses many domains.

These are among our quintessential servant leaders, whose stars rose to the heavens; on any given night, you can find them high in the sky. Seeing their stars, and that of all our awesome ancestors, we rejoice that the progenitors of the jubilee Beloved Community are from all ages, races, creeds, colors, and ages. We will raise them month by month, from year to year, in a Beloved Community hall of fame in hundreds of communities across the land.

Chapter 3

SoulScope®: Your Spiritual DNA

Knowing your SoulScope® makes all the difference in the world.

Symphony

Of

Unconditional

Love, as

Synchronized

Character,

Organized, and

Permeating

Earth

Chances are that you know your horoscope, but you don't know your SoulScope® profile. Your horoscope is about you and the starssomething external to you, therefore, not real. However, your SoulScope® is about you, based on a self-understanding you discern about this unique self, as gauged by the SoulScope® profiler, which it has been my challenge to design, and growing out of my search for the healing of my own soul.

It is like your spiritual DNA, and the SoulScope® profile is the only known system that can reliably help you know yourself, as the unique "one-among-nine" types of possibilities out of the entire human population, but absolutely unique, all by yourself. You know that you are a unique creation of divinity. Your rawness is your undifferentiated self, your rotten-ness, is more a creation of the demonic.

But, that's not the whole story.

The SoulScope® helps you understand how, in your redeemable state, you are the co-creation of divinity and developer of your own Soul.

The psychic networks have long extended a form of false hope to people, yielding questionable results and a tragically addicting effect for far too many. Any system that hooks people on their product or service and tricks them to spend their hard-earned bucks for another fix without fixing their yearning soul can and should be abandoned for the real thing.

SoulScope® makes two claims. First, it is not the real thing until you say it is. The proof is only in the eating of the pudding. Second, SoulScope® enables you to take charge of your own life, reduces your co-dependence on your weaker (demonic) self, and increases your reliance on your stronger (angelic) self.

The SoulScope® helps us understand and control both aspects of our being. It has the proven ability to help us know, own, blend, and use both aspects of our fundamental being-our rottenness and our redeemableness-in a synchronous oneness that lessens the dividedness of the soul, and helps us become awesome in our undivided oneness.

One hour with the SoulScope® can literally change one's life forever-is the claim being confidently made. Again, it isn't so until the person seeking to know the power of their own soul uses this tool, finds it to be true to the bold claims made, and says so.

The "footprints on the sands of time" about which the poet spoke are literally the soul prints of awesome ancestors. We have it when we know it. We know it when we live it.

SoulScope® Profiler

The SoulScope® Profiler was designed to assist individuals in understanding the strengths and weaknesses of their own unique temperament as one of nine possibilities, and empowers them through that greater self-understanding towards greater personal wholeness, interpersonal competence, cooperative teamwork, success, and life satisfaction.

It makes clear how the whole human race is fundamentally nine basic soul types, and your real living starts when you come to know your own type, and ultimately, that of the significant others in your life.

The SoulScope® personal profile analysis is designed to assist persons in self-understanding and the interpersonal dynamics for effective relationships and team building with others.

Soulscope®, Beyond the Enneagram

In order to clearly understand and use the SoulScope® Profiler, you begin with part one, by taking an Enneagram test.

SoulScope® Profiler: Type 7

SoulScope® profile number seven is being offered here in a bit more detail than how the other eight will be done in this document.

Once you complete part one (taking the Enneagram test), chances are that you will then be ready to learn how to show your own soul a little more tender love and care, and in the process, grow into a more gracious, powerful and productive human being.

The thesis behind this profile is that God awarded every human born a divine endowment as one of God's nine attributes or qualities of character. For the type-seven soul, that quality is joy. Along with that endowment, each human also receives one of the seven deadly sins as their original flaw, and in the case of the type-seven soul, that sin is gluttony. The whole human race is represented among the nine types, with none being better or worse than any other. It matters not what hand one is dealt; the difference is in how the game is played.

SoulScope® sevens tend to have a sunny disposition, walk the sunny side of the street, and feel happy as they sample one experience or relationship after another, never settling long enough to complete what they start, nor to make a real difference.

At their best, they can be very creative, upbeat high achievers, who make a big difference in important ways. They are at their best as they rise into their redeeming state or mood, finding joy in little achievements or big, by committing and staying with a more limited number of options. They range in mood, from a redeeming or joyful state at the high end, to a raw or average state, to a rotten or low mood (or state). At the high end, their divine endowment is joy; at the low end, their compulsion is gluttony. When type-seven souls operate from a rotten or low mood, their gluttony moves them in a downward spiral. They become dilettantes, fly-by-night, irresponsible, superficial operators.

On average, they tend to get themselves into more projects and commitments than they can possibly maintain, then become unfocused and ignore follow-through details, even as they plunge ahead into other projects.

Sevens get control of their moods over time, by practicing consciously the rhythm of thinking love, feeling joy, and doing peace. Each constitutes a special direction towards integration and innate health that sevens will come to pursue, as they commit to their own growth and the real solid achievement of their next level of success.

All the soul types go through some phase of these same type of moods, ranging from what I designated-high or redeeming, average or raw, to low or rotten. There is a protocol and path of direction for the healing of all nine soul types, and the SoulScope® Profiler offers each a similar process and path towards fulfillment.

As you put the care of your soul on the same level of importance as you place on anything else you value, then your sense of satisfaction in the personal, social, and professional areas of your life will take on new vitality.

We take better care of our automobiles, than our souls. Yes, our souls do break down from lack of love and care. Often, we find ourselves in the breakdown lane of life, and don't really know how we got there, or how to get up and out.

We try finding some peace with our souls, but most of the time, just as has been said, we "look for love in all the wrong places." Our soul hungers and thirsts for love; if we don't take the trouble to get the best quality love there is, we will fall for the wrong kind of soul food and drink, which neither nurtures nor satisfies.

Religions that teach that one must love him or herself before they can love others, nature, and God, are on the right track. And to get on course and get aligned with that endowment of love, we must invest loving time ("kairos" is the Greek term) into living time (which the Greeks called "chronos," from which we derive our term chronology). In short, what good is chronology without loveology?

At this point, allow me to congratulate you on taking your first step towards the care and feeding of your own soul. Other steps can involve further self-development as well as face-to-face consultation, which can be arranged.

As you go from step to step, you will discover that there are so many wonders about every self. And your self-discovery journey will not only enrich your life and the new satisfactions you will henceforth experience, but those around you will also share in those satisfactions.

The working hypothesis is that the Enneagram focused on your psychological underside, but the SoulScope® focuses on the upper-side of your soul, while acknowledging the reality of the underside. The soul needs the upper side and the underside, just like day needs the light and the darkness to be complete. The SoulScope® posits the theory that love (or its absence) is the defining value for humanity, and determines our wholeness, health, productivity, and happiness. The Enneagram, as it were, looks at the donut, but the SoulScope® looks at the hole. Maybe the 'hole' is in the soul. Does the soul need the hole? Does the hole give the soul breathing room? Quite likely. Stephen Wolinsky's, The Tao of Chaos: Essence and the Enneagram, sheds great light upon this matter.

Shakespeare said, "To be or not to be, that is the question." Maybe the most significant 'big question' for humanity is, "To love, or not to love?" It is a moment-by-moment, daily decision and choice. The choice is to love and be loved (or the choice to neglect or reject love, and not be loved). Learning by loving is to become re-connected into the unbroken circle oflove. To close the love loop is to enlarge the love circle.

The SoulScope® Profiler, a love meter of sorts, makes that formal assessment of one's life journey, in terms of predicament, present problems, inner conflict (or "stuck-ness"). The profiler also gauges one's total potential and how to activate it, and the resolution of the two in favor of their total forward progress. It has been designed to show how to make that assessment for soul, and suggests directions one might continue to take to increase love's felt presence in their own life, those around them, and the circle of health, love, and peace for individuals as well as the planet.

The essay by Henry Drummond, "The Greatest Thing in the World," appears in the index and is the basis for the following analysis of love, and the nine flavors of the fruit of the spirit, as lifted by New Testament writer Paul, in I Corinthians 13, and correlated with Galatians 5:22 and 23.

Death and life, as love misunderstood; later undersood, resurrected ...

1. "Love suffereth long ..."
   EightLove is love waiting, as Patience.
   Fruit of spirit is longsuffering; fatal flaw is lust.
2. " ... and is kind ..."
   FourLove is love active, as Kindness.
3. "Love vaunteth not itself, is not puffed up ..."
   FiveLove is love hiding, as Humility.
4. " ... Love envieth not..."
   SixLove is love in competition, as generosity.
5. "Doth not behave itself unseemly ..."
   SevenLove, is love in trifles, as courtesy.
6. " ... Seeketh not her own..."
TwoLove is love in service, as compassion.
7. "Is not easily provoked ..."

OneLove is good temper, as self-control.

8. "... Thinketh no evil ..."

ThreeLove is love as Goodness/Guilelessness.

9. "Rejoiceth not in iniquity; but rejoiceth in the truth"

NineLove is love as Peace.

"Beareth all things, believeth all things, hopeth all things, endureth all things..."

"Love never Faileth: but whether there be prophecies, they shall fail; whether there be tongues, they shall cease, whether there be knowledge, it shall vanish away."

10. Love resurrected: conversation within the family of Father Abraham, and other believers, living in a society based on organized lovelessness (Fritz Kunkel).

The resurrection of love awakens in us the memory of love, when God serenaded each human being with a doxology of praise.

At our conception, which was the inception of our own spot of grace, a divine endowment was given, both image and shadow.

And the image of life and love is destined to outshine the shadow of fear and death, which translates into:

- Compassion overcoming pride;
- Joy overcoming gluttony;
- Peace overcoming apathy;
- Goodness overcoming deceit;
- Kindness overcoming envy;
- Gentleness overcoming greed;
- Faith overcoming anxiety;
- Patience overcoming anger; and
- Endurance overcoming lust.

These indeed, make a revolution in love, for love, through love! Halleluiah ... Amen ... Shalom ... Asalam alakum ... Amen.

Here are a few topics to consider in this conversation: life, death, abuse, violence, crime, death, energy, light, resurrection, memory, shadow, fear, image, grace, endowment, destiny, awakening, consciousness, love (others).

Chapter 4

Education Reform: First Things First

Toxic education and polluted souls: the critical role of the black church in helping reform underperforming schools, and saving the soul of America 's youth.

Reversing the Jail Trail begins with preventing children and youth from being caught up in the criminal justice system in the first place. Prevention is a key strategy, and successful schooling is the first plank in such a platform. For inner-city communities, the church is a key player. Making sure our young people finish high school requires the kind of after school care that the traditional ethnic day schools have long demonstrated.

It starts with the black church. The first step involves inner-city pastors, and spiritual leaders.

Organizational Model for a Jubilee Pastor's Roundtable

The model suggested is that of inner-city community coalition groups functioning in tandem, around the broad common agenda areas of critical need in those communities whose first focus will be the critical role of the black church and its communities in reforming underperforming schools.

This is a necessary component of putting our children and youth on the high road towards their own choice-filling future, and away from the abuse, crime, violence, and death, so endemic to most inner city environments. The writer is indebted to Benjamin Hickman Wright, Jr. and the late H. Naylor Fitzhugh, one of the awesome ancestors, already cited, for many of the main ideas on which this model is built.

A regional jubilee pastor's roundtable functions as a coalition of church-based, and related pre-professional and professional organizations, which will oversee the development of the total agenda for the inner-city community by working with coalition groups across the region, to forge for each year, our goals, objectives, timelines, and resources, and a periodic regional forum for information sharing, fellowship, inspiration, and joint action around goals that are regionwide. These conceivably might include: • National and regional economic analysis and forecast reports

- National and regional economic development
- Financial institution building
- Land reclamation and production
- Religious cooperation
- Food cooperatives
- Energy cooperatives
- Prison ministry of jubilee
- New outlook and inspiration for youth
- Solidarity against any form of attack anywhere, and
- Others ...

The overall organization would be a mass-based coalition of coalitions. It is hereby suggested that at least four clusters of coalitions are formed, including a religious coalition, of which the pastor's roundtable would be simply the convening arm.

Others clusters would be: civic, community, and political; business, finance, and economics; educational, cultural, and social; and the clergy-based coalition or cluster.

A pastor's roundtable would function in each city, and all four clusters would convene in that respective place.

The session would be the mass assembly, called by the roundtable, but the research, planning, and proposal work would be done within each cluster. The roundtable would elect a general chairperson, (which would be a rotating position every three or six months) and a chair and co-chair for each cluster area.

Such an overall movement would focus upon the needs and opportunities for building strength within and among all the areas cited.

What will they do and how will they do it?

Recommendations

1. That the worthy, challenging goal of attaining economic parity for black people must studiously, deliberately, address the needs of black people on a broad basis, serving the crying needs of the masses as well as the interests of the "talented tenth" among us. Indeed, this effort should command genuine service inputs from a "talented tenth" honestly seeking to raise the conditions of the community that has long nurtured the more fortunate brothers and sisters. They would enflesh Mrs. Mary McLeod Bethune's legacy of love by following her example and advice, to "lift as we climb."

2. That the goal of economic parity for black people must command the attention and energies of a wide range of major organizations focused regionally and locally, devoted to constructive programming for dramatic improvement of the black condition in the region, including, but not limited to the following:

- Civil rights organizations
- Business organizations
- Religious organizations
- Educational organizations
- Political action organizations
- Welfare organizations
- Professional organizations
- Fraternal organizations
- Workers organizations
- Student organizations, and
- Legislative organizations

3. That steps must be taken forthwith to structure an effective working coalition, or consortium, of regional and local organizations, whose prima-

ry purpose will be to deliberate, discuss, and debate key issues in the cause of educational and economic parity. Such a coalition would have as its basic objectives:

a. Identification/articulation of the critical goals to be achieved.

b. Definition of the time-spans within which the achievement of these goals will be sought.

c. Examining the various action/program options-available, proposed, and/or needed-and adopting coalition positions of those programs on which unanimity can be developed.

d. Maintain/operate a two-way flow of information/ recommendations between the coalition and its constit- uents, to expand/ increase the representative-ness of coalition positions, on the one hand, and the energetic support of these positions-at the local level, on the other.

4. That in the interest of span-of-control, the regional groups com- prising the coalition should be as inclusive as possible; in other words, the coalition will—to a considerable degree—itself constitute a coalition of or- ganizational coalitions.

5. That coalition's actions should carefully and studiously be confined to the unique roles defined above; that the coalition should studiously avoid impinging upon specific program thrusts of constituent organizations.

6. That the financing of the coalition should come initially—and per- haps solely—from the constituent organizations; that the coalition should not assume a posture of a super organization competing with constituent organizations for financing.

7. That the coalition itself adopts a low-profile posture; that public vis- ibility be focused, rather, upon the constituent organizations and their con- stituencies.

8. That the coalition could operate through task forces dealing out of

and, with each of the four or five major areas of coalition concerns, the overall and the clusters.

9. That in order to insure organizational continuity, responsibility, and stability, membership of the coalition should be on an organizational basis, primarily.

10. That the coalition's executive leadership could be vested in an executive council possibly composed of the general, the co-chair persons, and the task force leadership teams; and the general chairpersonship should rotate.

The coalition's primary objective: capturing the mind of each student so that they become educated and productive citizens ... stop talking about it and just do it!

In partnership, several national organizations have teamed up and have discovered what will prove to be the most powerful and efficacious education and prevention approach yet found. For the first time, a research-proven outside-in approach has combined with the most effective inside-out approach to produce something far beyond anything that has been attempted to date. We believe that this combined approach will achieve the results, and with it the answers, that this Administration and the American people seek.

People want answers to the problems facing this nation's children and its schools. They are frustrated. They point fingers and blame others. There is a lack of respect and understanding for each other. There is high teacher turnover. People no longer want to enter the teaching profession. For the students, there is a disconnectedness, disenfranchisement, low academic achievement. This leads to abuse, violence, crime, drugs and death.

The antidote is connectedness. It is bringing people together—but not in the usual way. It brings them together in such a way where they can see exactly what they need to do to create healthy, constructive, and lasting change. It is a recognition that it all begins within the minds of the students and leads to creating educated, productive citizens.

Goals

We believe that the only goals worth seeking are results-oriented. The goals for this effort are to improve academic achievement as measured by educational assessments, to increase school attendance, and to reduce student dropouts and violent, abusive, delinquent, and inappropriate, acting out behavior. In short, students will want to be in school. They will drop out less. They will act out less. Teachers will be less stressed and more productive in their jobs, leading to better morale and lower teacher turnover. Administrators will run more peaceful, higher-achieving schools. Parents will be more supportive of school and will participate more; they will be less abusive and more supportive of their children. The community will experience less crime and violence.

What the field and this nation has been missing, and what sets this approach apart:

Until now, we have not understood the essence of what changes people. We have been so focused on the complexity that we have not seen the simplicity, and in simplicity lies the true power of change.

FACT: No matter what elaborate, effective assessment tools are developed, unless all players understand how to work together to create the best environments in which all students can thrive and perform at their best, it will not amount to much.

FACT: If students' minds do not function at the optimal level, their assessment scores will be lower than they could be.

FACT: No matter what so-called great programs are created, if students' thinking has not changed—in fact, if the thinking of teachers, administrators, and coaches has not changed—no behavior change will occur because behavior is always and indisputably the direct result of people's thinking.

FACT: No matter what so-called great educational efforts are created, if students-and teachers, administrators, coaches, and parentsdo not emerge being guided by their own wisdom and common sense, they will still behave in ways counter to their own long-term best interests and this nation's best interests as citizens. This combined approach attacks these head-on.

Never before has an outside-in approach been combined with an inside-out approach. Both have been boiled down to their essence to make it simple enough for anyone to grasp.

The Outside-In Approach (and its achieved results):

The Global Center for Student Aspirations has gained national and international recognition for its research-based development of eight conditions that foster aspirations and for its innovative approach to helping schools and parents obtain and incorporate students' perspectives and needs into targeted programs and overall educational reform efforts.

The center, with over two decades of research, has identified eight conditions that affect the development of student aspirations and ultimately student achievement on multiple levels. The work of the global center is to establish conditions in school, which will provide an environment in which each and every student can reach their fullest potential.

The Global Center for Student Aspirations is a resource for leadership, research and interventions aimed at improving educational environments. It responds to the tremendous need and interest in the validity and potential of student aspirations as an essential component of academic achievement, student retention and overall school improvement.

The center focuses its research and programs on eight conditions that encourage and foster student aspirations. Researchers working in schools searching for the factors that positively influence development of student aspirations identified these conditions. They are:

- Belonging
- Heroes
- Sense of accomplishment
- Fun and excitement

- Curiosity and creativity
- Spirit of adventure
- Leadership and responsibility
- Confidence to take action

The first step in establishing the eight conditions is to be committed to doing something, to making even the smallest change. Be committed to listening to student voices and to taking positive action. Be committed to finding and fulfilling the promise and potential each student possesses.

Several years ago, the center surveyed over 100,000 students in order to gain insights into their perceptions or school. This ambitious project, based on their eight conditions, unveiled their views on the conditions in schools that affect their aspirations, attitudes, and ultimately their academic achievement.

Two key themes consistently arise from the findings of this unparalleled research. First, students believe in their ability to improve and that, with hard work, they can reach their goals. Unfortunately, the second major finding is that students are not inspired in the presenttoday or next week-to recognize options or to extend the necessary effort to reach the goals they envision. In short, students are thinking about their future, and believe they will be successful, but they need inspiration, encouragement, and support to target and work purposely toward their objectives.

Whether we are educators, parents, pastors, community members, business people or policy makers, we should all share one common interest and responsibility-to help students reach their fullest potential. Each ofus can help shape the aspirations of a (each and every) student, and, thus, the future of society.

The Inside-Out Approach

In areas replete with violence, abuse, crime, drugs, gangs, teen pregnancy, unemployment, an approach called health realization has shown dramatic reductions in these problems of from 60% to 80% (Pransky, Mills, Sedgeman & Blevens, 1997). Among students in these areas, academic achievement has improved significantly. Health realization points people within themselves to discover their own innate mental health, wisdom and common sense. It helps them see that this state comes naturally when people's minds are calm, relaxed, and clear. It helps them see that the only thing keeping them from experiencing it at any moment is the kind of thinking that occurs when people's minds are stressed, agitated, busy, fearful, angry, depressed, in low moods, etc.

This approach helps people see how they are ruled by their thinking unless they see what is going on. It is not a cognitive approach in that it does not focus on the content of people's thinking or how to change already-thought thoughts; instead, it simply helps people see the mechanism at work behind their experience. When people see how it all works within them, their lives change-for the better. Thought is the missing link in creating change. When this is seen people's minds begin to function at a more optimal level.

This effort can begin in six to eight demonstration sites throughout the country, such as: Houston, TX, Providence, RI; Tampa, FL; Richmond, VA; Charleston, WV; Nashville, TN; Bemidji, MN; Bristol or St. Johnsbury, VT; Appalachia and East St. Louis, IL; or San Jose, CA. Or it could focus on half-dozen cities in the New England Region.

Church and Community Development Associates is a faith-based, African-American approach to total self development, working through its Lamp Stand Institute in this effort. This model is that of an inner city community coalition of groups functioning in tandem, around the broad common agenda areas of the critical needs of its families. It is convened by a pastor's roundtable, which functions in tandem with other coalitions focusing on the needs and opportunities for building strength among those devoted to the spiritual, economic, educational, civic, social and general betterment of its communities. This particular approach is composed of a kind of coalition of coalitions, but also works with other coalitions outside the African-American church and community. Its core activities are focused within inner city and related rural communities.

A consortium including the Global Center for Student Aspirations, the faith-based Jubilee National Fellowship, and the Northeast Health Realization Institute, has been at work to respond to the suggested demonstration cities, or any others where churches and communities are ready to work for this kind of educational Reform.

A Modern-Day Mountaneer Miracle: Just The Right Kind of Medicine.

As an outsider looking in on West Virginia a few years ago, I was both amazed and delighted! At Charleston, Morgantown, and indeed all across the state of West Virginia, a major, modem-day miracle percolates.

The Robert Byrd Health Sciences' Medical School at the University of West Virginia created a crown jewel for turning around middle and high school students from a life of un-productivity, and its attendant social costs, into high performing successful learners, now competent and caring contributors to their society and to its tax coffers.

This crown jewel is the almost 10-year-old Health Science and Technology Academy program, called HSTA. At a time when the national will is turning against the poor educational results that have left a majority of our public school students behind, HSTA may well be the cornerstone for achieving the kind of school success that has so long eluded our students and teachers all across America, and for which we all have waited so long. It may well be that this is the very model that gives us the will and the way, to truly, leave no child behind.

One very critical component of the highly successful HSTA program is the new understanding afforded to students, teachers, and parents; and a new mindset about life and learning-which is affiliated with the Sydney Banks Institute for Innate Health. The program was inspired by Dr. Robert D' Alessandri, then vice president and dean for health sciences at the University of West Virginia Medical School; directed by Dr. Ann Chester; and chaired by businessman Steve Starks.

Now with the extraordinary results achieved by HSTA students, families, and teachers, and with those critical new outcomes carefully documented, the groundwork is laid for a national replication of this highly successful model, to benefit under-performing students and schools all across America, starting with a few carefully chosen sites for initial planning and implementation. The team is in place for this task.

The quick mobilization of the required resources can put School Systems on a fast track toward meeting not only the new rules and requirements for accountability, but also the reasonable expectation of students and families that with cooperation on the part of all, Schools will do what Schools are designed to do, "bring out the best in all our students," an effort HSTA is carrying forth across the State of West Virginia, and now can make across America.

If at 14, Johnny can't read, but is fortunate enough to meet HSTA, and then ten years later, at 24, has become, Johnny, the Excellent Teacher of Reading (or any other discipline), wouldn't we call this a modem day miracle ? The time is now upon us to let this Modem Day Mountaineer Miracle, flow across the nation into the lives of all the Johnnies and Joannas! When do we get started?

An Alternate Initiative that Leverages the Mainstream

We are told by experts that most teen-age pregnancies, drive-by shootings, drug dealings, and most forms of abuse, violence, crime, death and ill health, among our youth, take place each day, between the hours of 3:00 and 6:00 p.m., as a general rule.

This grim reality makes it all the more compelling that faith-inspired organizations and their partners undertake a major after-school campaign that will enhance the learning process already underway in day school. This undertaking engages elementary, middle school and high school youth during after-school hours, in activities that will also add civility to their common life, and nobility of service and economic viability to their daily living. One initial milestone will be the annual, citywide rites of passage for our boys and girls who will have undergone the prescribed course for this level of their presentation to society, and will be as their grandest birthday party to date.

The Carver-Anderson-Fuller After School-School School System, A3S, is being born out of the artistic genius of the late great, Marian Anderson and the scientific genius of the late great George Washington Carver, and R. Buckminster Fuller.

The community giving birth to this school knows the value and necessity of saving our youth, and redeeming our total community. It knows equally well, the necessary role of the mind and the spirit and the soul of our awesome ancestry. How shall they learn (love of truth; self; others; nature; and the love source) except they are taught by those who first of all love truth, others (especially those they would teach, nature; and the love source) as well as themselves.

It is the spirit of Carver, Anderson and Fuller which motivates the founders of this school A3S, in love of truth, humanity, and the community of learners.

The A3S will be modeled after a combination of educational institutions, in which the Roland Hayes and the Duke Ellington Schools of Music help shape the music component. Mrs. Anderson's life journey shares the environmental topography of our current inner city youth, and her choices mirror the battle for excellence being added to their natural endowments.

The contribution of "Bucky" Fuller to science and technology puts him heads and shoulders above almost anybody who has combined the blessings and the rigors of science for the good of humanity.

We will model those educational institutions doing the best job at present for inner city youth, and their communities, of bringing them into the 21st century of technological necessity and competence. The net effect of such a school will be to raise the level of character, competence, and compassion in all the members of this learning community, including but not limited to the youth who study there day and night.

This after-school campaign will also include two additional components. First, entrepreneurship will be the foundation of its link to viability of living and nobility of service. Second, martial arts will be the main athletic expression, and will bring into play, the civility of societies in our shared and collective lives.

A pastor's roundtable could launch this after-school operation and raise an endowment for its enhancement, and launch it as a partnership between all relevant sectors.

The New England region is blessed in having the creative leadership, and proven expertise of Robert Winfrey, founder and former director of the Roland Hayes School of Music, in Boston. He brings in addition, a fine working relationship with the famed Berklee School of Music, which is being invited into this partnership.

The A3S envisions components involving music, computers, entrepemeurship, and martial arts, and will have as its defining framework, the blending of student aspirations and character enhancement.

The A3S Group is being led by a community coalition exploratory effort, and does anticipate a close working relationship with the Roland Hayes and the Berklee Schools of Music in Boston, and other kindred operations around the country.

An early part of the planning for this school has already involved an intensive "meeting of the minds" by living colleagues of Mrs. Anderson and Mr. Fuller, in addition to educationists, community participants, scientists, potential business partners, university partners, school administration partners, and members of the philanthropic community.

The general question now to be probed is: How can an A3S, of music, leadership, technology, entrepreneurship and martial arts put an end to abuse, violence, crime death, and ill-health and mark a new start for the village as a Universal Beloved Community learning center?

Every inner-city and rural community, needs to ponder this question for their own community, and in the process, forge the necessary alliance of human and non-human resources to truly work together, so as to truly leave no child behind!

Part Two:
Hope Beyond Despair

"Only God Knows" Ezekiel 37:3b

Chapter 5

Negative Forces Preventing Development

As an Amafrican, have you ever considered how future history books might record and sum up why and how black folk almost missed the boat to freedom? I say almost only as an act of faith. Let's put it in its worse possible light. How might future history books, record the reasons why black people as a people got destroyed from the earth. I still mean almost; however, one sequence might go that when the Martin Luther King movement shook the chains off their hands, feet and minds that black folk continued to act as though their minds, hands, feet and hearts were still chained. After the chains were gone, suppose the black folk mainly just sat there as though in a daze, not knowing what to do with themselves. At one minute standing up talking loud and incoherent, and at another time, acting out this chaotic mindset.

For a few moments, let me try to be the person to explain this type behavior. Let's see if there is a new type of doctor in the house-if you please-who can give the dynamics of the situation, help the patients understand what's happening to them, by sifting out their thoughts and behavior and then help them get a new grip on self and remold their own world, according to the new and saner understanding now achieved.

I guess I really believe that the numbness was really in the mind, although not a numskull. Like a leg, or an arm that goes to sleep on you, your mind too, sometimes has to be awakened. Once it's awakened, it's the same mind as before. However, it has a new mindset, a new framework for understanding, and a better reality orientation for action and behavior. It is really as a doctor of organization that I want to perform my analysis, diagnosis, then prognosis, on the black community with its negative forces, which prevent economic and community development.

My preliminary observation tells me that there are two main types of negative forces working on the black community. It has some very peculiar symptoms. Mainly I have already described some of them. The result is that the community that has so much to gain from working together in unity, seems to really love and enjoy disunity. Why is it that a people who really need each other to lean on for their ability to survive together are a people who kill each other off as though they were enemies at war, whether in Los Angeles, or Liberia? Sometimes such behavior is exhibited by blood brothers and sisters. But, blood or no blood, these forces are quite confusing and contradictory.

At the same time, we do want to understand this abnormal behavior in the light of its dysfunctionality, its un-workability, its craziness, and how that prevents real economic progress from taking place. In fact, this dysfunctional behavior sometimes will interrupt the very path of sure progress itself, and at the point that the victory is almost clinched, turn it into a path of defeat. It's like the proverbial cow, giving a bucket full of milk and then kicking it over.

It is the kind of behavior that seems to prefer losing to winning, to prefer death to life, and to prefer poverty instead of fulfillment. These are among the negative forces, which prevent economic and community development and insures that communities stay as they are and get worse, as soon as possible. How do we make sense out of such nonsense? What are these negative forces that prevent development? And how does the black community overcome them?

Of the two major categories of illnesses, preventing positive health and growth in economics in the black community, one is well-known to doctors of organizational science and the other is not so well known. It may well be that mainly a black organizational development mentality will help us recognize and understand the second and the way the two interact with each other. Let me be clearer. In order to have you understand where I am trying to go, I now have to throw in two fairly unknown economic terms, which relate to critical variables and factors to be controlled.

If we are to bring the organizational sickness under control, and create health and economic growth, the terms to be understood are endogenous and exogenous. Let us look at the definitions as given in the *Penguin Dictionary of Economics*, by Banner, Baxter and Reed.

Slaves as Descendants in their Own Demise: The Endogenous Variable, Own or Be Owned

According to the dictionary, the endogenous variable is classified as a variable whose value is to be determined by forces operating within the model under consideration. For example, in a model of the market for wheat, the price of wheat is an endogenous variable because it is determined by the forces of supply and demand incorporated in the model itself.

The variables to be understood, to sift out the negative forces preventing development of the black community, are both endogenous and exogenous. Sometimes there is a thin line between them.

Let us now turn to our field of observation of the organizational and community behavior for our analysis. The endogenous factors are those that relate to the way the black community within itself functions against itself and its own best interest. And the exogenous will deal with the variable of racism and its windward side from the point of its residual effect on black social behavior. Even after the racist quits, his effects remain. Our understanding of this phenomenon must accord with the facts; otherwise, we delude ourselves with the wrong conclusions and suffer there from.

Black people, in their organizational and interpersonal relations, have a set of dysfunctional behavior patterns that we can refer to as hang-ups. In terms of organizational behavior and interpersonal behavior, the list is too long. The seven dimensions are:

- A low survivability competence
- A failure to use well our present resources
- High levels of inter-group rivalries
- High levels of mistrust and suspicion
- A high level of psychological dependency on (the man) even while disclaiming the same
- A high level of economic dependency on (the man)
- A low level of independence and interdependence within our own black life and organization.

The external circumstances of our seven levels of entrapment seem not to be more problematic than these seven social and psychological barriers, just enumerated. In fact, these seven barriers to economic and community health and viability, may well be the social and psychological glue that holds the seven circles of entrapment into place. There are some rather substantial reasons for these hang-ups that we have just explained and they will be touched on very briefly.

Firstly, the ghetto functions as an economic disincentive system, such that rather than rewarding positive action and behavior, it gets penalized (How and why our children "diss" education).

On the other hand, the same system rewards negativity, crime, and in-action. It is the same sense in which Congressman William Clay, pointed out in an article published by the *Boston Globe*, on December the 21, 1971, entitled, "Economics of Hustling a Ghetto Blight." Basically, it is the very economic structure of the ghetto itself and its setup, sanctioned and operated by powers outside the ghetto. Clay refers to it as an underworld sub-economy. "That sub-economy is based on illegal rackets and other underworld activities, which flourish in black communities and are completely acceptable to the white majority."

Further, he makes it clear how the working dude is seen as square when he brings home a net of six dollars a day, and the hustler is able to make up to two and three-hundred dollars per day through illegal activities which again are acceptable to the white controllers of the ghetto. Moreover, Congressman Clay gave his own antidote for this condition of what he calls economic hustling. "The alternative to this fluid financial modus operandi is to pump business and industry on a large scale into the ghettos with a guaranteed income for every family plus crash vocational education programs and on the job training.

Part of this picture is also, that which drugs and crime play in its incapacitation of black communities. While it is known that these conditions exist with the sanctions if not also the participation of the white power structure, it is inconceivable, that these same conditions could continue if the black community stood up denounced and ejected that way of doing things. The question of how is never the ultimate question once people have found the will and the determination to accomplish whatever they feel they must accomplish. That ultimately also comes down to the problem of leadership in the ghetto.

That is the second side of the ghetto disincentive system and the economics of hustling. It is the network of social service type organizations, which have their very life and budgets at the sufferance of the very forces, which—intentionally or not—perpetuate the ghetto system. Such organizations show little entrepreneurial drive although some do in finding a way as an organization to survive, without having to go time and again with monkey cup in hand to the very forces which desire and achieve the status quo of the inner city and will profit from the same, in some way.

Once, the major problems of that type approach are worked out, massive responses from black people are likely. Since, black community organization executives meet each other in the revolving door of the same business and foundation interests competing for the same scarce social service dollar it is not in their organizational interest to have genuine cooperation. They then must bump each other off to reduce the level of competition for that scarce social service dollar. There are signs that this may be changing with more emphasis being placed on the need for collaboration, although it is often collaboration for the same level of resources, and in many case, a reduced dollar.

These organizations are surviving on the crumbs of grants and seem not inclined to change rather than define for themselves a new level of economic growth and urban development in which they could participate around the strengths and contributions which their organizations could make to that process taking assignment and receiving fees for their productive input to that process. Once, we have the "on the mark, get set, go" signal, billions of dollars are likely to be spent in helping rebuild the cities and construct brand new towns on land presently vacant.

All development efforts of this magnitude have what is called hard investment dollars which investors expect and have every right to get back and to receive interest on in the meantime. Now there is also, what I shall call the "soft social overhead dollar," which must work along with the hard dollar in development efforts. Such social service organizations must begin now to ready themselves for competently participating in the social overhead work as part of the development process in building new towns. In addition, the reparations and restitution dollars will be a vital part of enabling black institutions ourselves, to fix what's broke among our own people.

Fundamental to everything we are saying about these negative patterns, economics is at the base. This is especially true at the level of the traditional hostilities between the black masses and the black classes, where they refer derogatorily to each other as bourgeois and crazy niggers, etc. The point remains the same. If the black classes could help design and set-up the preconditions for the takeoff to a new economic ball game, in which the black masses had real new opportunities for participation, each group would then begin to understand the mutual stake they have in each other's well-being, made operative by this new ball game.

The masses know that their anger during the sixties and seventies, in the street, loosened-up Americans attitudes and a few more crumbs flowed.

But the black classes were the real beneficiaries or so it would seem. A new economic framework is now in order in which black professionals use their skills and talents to work helping put together what they both need to be independent and interdependent eventually. Such effort in time would certainly be jointly affirmed by the masses and the classes, and could benefit both, and proportionately.

The variable to control in this case with all of the say in their own hand is around the incentive pie, how to make it big enough for everyone to get a slice and the refusal to used as hustlers whether of crime or of social services. When black America gets this right, it will build its own sub-economy as a beloved economy, leveraging and multiplying its undisciplined annual black dollar flow of $850 billion, into that disciplined, non-violent, beloved economy.

The Exogenous Variable!

The exogenous variable is defined as a variable that-although playing an important part in a model-is determined by forces outside the model and is unexplained by it. For example, in our model of the wheat, weather conditions may play an important part in determining the supply and the price of the wheat, but the model itself does not try to explain what determines weather conditions.

We have already said that it deals with how racism seems to continue working on us even after the racists quit. I translate it to mean, if racism doesn't stop you, then fear surely will, given the way we function in the city. There are conditions under which fear becomes a confederate with racism to work to this person's defeat where racism alone would be unable to accomplish that result.

In a situation where the main barriers have been racism in the past, and now for the sake of argument, let's say an individual has a 50 percent chance or possibility of success, now a fighting chance, a real chance. Suppose he or she had not gotten the clue, the chances have now gone from maybe 0%

or 10%—which is pretty chancy—up to say 45% or 65% which would be a pretty good chance. But, the person does not perceive that his chances have changed, and he refuses to check it out to make the effort. Where the person's effort in the past have been met with a closed door, and continual rebuffs he tends to fear making a new effort.

In a discussion, of whether a person makes realistic efforts towards success or failure, J.T. Atkins' theory is informative. "Under what conditions might persons accustomed to failure be encouraged towards more realistic goal setting and efforts designed to be success oriented? This question goes to the heart of the need for the model and defines a core area of that activity. Atkins sets forth two sets of variables or questions, which explain this behavior.

1. To what extent does the individual in sizing up the task before him expect that his performance will lead on to the goal of success?
2. How attractive does success at this particular activity appear to the individual? That is, how much of an incentive does it present, even if it is something that he knows he could do, what is it worth to do it?"

The formula is expressed as $(T=M \times P \times I)$ and expresses the strength of ones' motivation to achieve, or tendency to really try to achieve. The (T) stands for, the tendency to put forth efforts whether success oriented or failure oriented; the (M) is the person's motive profile, the strength of his motive how he tends to respond, which he carries with him like his face, from situation to situation; the (P) is the strength of expectancy or the probability of success. Sometimes, a person accomplishes the unexpected because he did not know that it was supposed to be impossible. That's the probability of success factor. And the (I) equals the incentive value of the effort.

We believe that in the black community, the probability of success factor, is the controlling one, often over looked. The whole formula adds up to the kind of effort that the person will put together as determined by all these variables. For the person motivated by the fear of failure that has experienced continued defeat and failure in the things they have attempted that are of importance to themselves, the question around the tendency to try is vastly different. Just as the tendency to approach success is at its strongest when there is a moderate probability of success that is at least 50%, so is the tendency to avoid failure when the task appears to be of intermediate difficulty.

The motivator of action where failure results is anxiety, and a tendency to withdraw from the situation or challenge. Thus, the motive to avoid failure and expectation of failure function to steer the individual away from success oriented activities and directly to the kinds of action steps, which insure that he's going to fail. In other words, when he is motivated from a fear of failure, it almost programs him unerringly in the direction of failure as though failure were his goal. The increased ability which one achieves by realistically assessing the external constraints to his success, the assessment of his own personal motive profile for realistically understanding his own behavior, can help him moderate his risk taking, so that it is appropriate to the new level of his last success.

From there on it is practice all the way. Nothing overcomes the fear of failure like the realistic assessment suggested and the continual practice of increasing successes. It's like going from one small success to one larger success until finally to a real significant success. This is true for both the individual and the society. It has already been well said, "nothing succeeds like success."

The testimony of the old black bard was "my dungeon shook and my chains fell off." We too, know that with the work of King, allies, the dungeon of racism in our time shook and our chains fell off. We just know it, deep down we know it, but are we really sure whether we can walk or not? And maybe later we'll start thinking about running. A new step carefully planned, in a direction that really matters and calculating every key variable that has to be manipulated, can insure new and important successes.

VIRGIL WOOD

It's like the first time you drove a car all by yourself, it just seemed that there were at least three dozen key factors that you had to control, and before you know it, you drive the car without really even concentrating away from the things on your mind that are really important. That's one small example of how we overcome fear almost on a daily basis. Yes, one day black people just might stretch forth their wings; they just might try to fly.

Chapter 6

Malcom X: Faith and Hope, Beyond Despair

There was an important interchange between Malcolm X and King, some explicit, but mostly implicit. Many believe that in the course of time, they became more like each other. In the SoulScope® venue, with each doing serious soul work, especially in their final phase, there is some justification for the thought that each moved in the end, towards a position in the middle of both of their original positions on race and the change that was called for by each of them.

Complexity of Malcolm

Locating Malcolm X on the SoulScope® range is no easy matter. Malcolm changed during the course of his life, not as most people change, as they grow, but Malcolm went through a series of transformations. He was aware of this, as he states in page 339 of his autobiographical work: "My whole life had been a chronology of changes" (The Autobiography of Malcolm X, As Told to Alex Haley. New York: Ballantine Books, 1965). For this reason, classifying his personality type is difficult, to say the least. Mere classification cannot capture the complexity of the man.

Malcolm would likely have agreed with the above statement. When his autobiography neared completion, he said to Alex Haley, the writer who would pull the book together: "A writer is what I want, not an interpreter" (pg. 456). It was Malcolm's intention that his life speak for itself, without interpretation, because he felt his life needed none. Arguably, it doesn't.

Malcolm X was angry. His story leaves one with little doubt that his anger was justifiable. Like everyone, he made mistakes in his life. He was excessive in almost everything he did, whether that was hustling or promoting the Nation of Islam. Yet, despite his faults, Malcolm was, above all, a man—as Ossie Davis so eloquently pointed out in his eulogy of Malcolm on page 460 of his autobiography: He stood up, and "scared hell" out of everyone, black, white, Christian and Jew, with that " ... shocking zing of fire-and-be-damned-to-you style." Back then, in the late-fifties and early-sixties, shocking people into their senses was required, and Malcolm knew this. He was a man who did what was required, when it was required, whatever the consequences or imbalances that resulted.

What Soul Type Might We Assign to Malcolm X?

Malcolm appears as a soul-type six when measured against the Enneagram system. As just indicated, smug classifications of this man are fraught with peril. Despite this, it will become clear how it is possible that personality type six, the Loyalist, applies to him. For it turned out to be Malcolm X's blinding loyalty to one person, the man he called the "honorable Elijah Muhammad," that became the singular mark of his life. An Enneagram evaluation explains the unquestioning nature of this loyalty well. It is in loyalty to Elijah Muhammad that Malcolm did all of his professional work, and in loyalty that Malcolm's entire psychological process was rooted during his rise to fame.

True, Malcolm's loyalty was only one facet of his character. He had aspects of the leader (type eight), the thinker (type five), the reformer (type one), and even the status seeker (type three) interwoven into his personality, sprinkled in even amounts. That was a function of the man's remarkable complexity. However, it was the blindness of his loyalty: the complete, uncritical acceptance of the ideas and the person of Elijah Muhammad that leaps out of Malcolm's life story. It is this trait in Malcolm's character that leads us to place him as a six.

Let us review some of the traits of the six in the Enneagram system, before looking at Malcolm's life in depth. The Enneagram type six is described in Don Richard Riso's book, Personality Types: Using the Enneagram for

Self-Discovery or review the material on the website, SoulScope.com under "What's My Type?"

Soul Type Six

According to Riso, sixes—like the other personality types in the "doing" triad (i.e., fives and sevens}—are full of anxiety: They are reactive, fluttering from one state to another very quickly. Sixes are ambivalent: the two distinct sides of their personalities oscillate between aggressive and dependent tendencies. And, to make matters more complicated, sixes are not only ambivalent toward others, they are ambivalent toward themselves. They like themselves one moment, and then disparage themselves the next, feeling inferior to others. They have confidence and then seem hopeless, as if they could not do anything without the help of someone else.

All three personality types in the doing triad have a problem with anxiety, but sixes, as the primary type, have the greatest problem with it. They are the type, which is most conscious of anxiety—"anxious that they are anxious."

There are times when they may not seem to be anxious at all since when they react to anxiety, average sixes can be highly aggressive and belligerent. Nevertheless, anxiety underlies everything, either as an expression of it, or as a reaction to it.

Role of Authority Figures

Sixes are full of contradictions: they are emotionally dependent on others, yet do not reveal much of themselves. They worship authority, yet fear it; they are obedient yet disobedient, fearful of aggression, yet sometimes highly aggressive themselves. They search for security, yet feel insecure. They are likable and endearing, yet can be mean and hateful. They believe in traditional values, yet may subvert those values. They want to escape punishment, yet may bring it on themselves. Sixes are full of contradictions because anxiety makes them ricochet from one psychological state to another. And in response to anxiety, sixes look to an authority to put their anxiety to rest.

For sixes, security comes from a rock-of-ages allegiance to an authority outside the self, which they can obey. Sixes want to feel protected and secure by having something more powerful than they guiding them. IBM will do, but so will the Communist Party, the Republican Party, or the church. The doctrines that sixes believe in are important to them, but not as important as having someone to believe in.

Childhood Origins

As a result of their childhood experiences, sixes identify positively with their fathers or a father figure. As children, sixes wanted the security of being approved by their fathers and felt anxious if they did not receive it. As they grew up, their positive identification with their fathers shifted to identification with more abstract father figures, such as civil authorities or belief systems from which they could obtain security.

As children, sixes learned to feel secure by trying to please their fathers in whatever ways were demanded. They learned to follow the rules of the home and to become responsible members of society by being obedient, approved members of their first group, their families. But in doing so, they learned that value exists outside themselves in the authority who will reward them if they do what they are told. If they do not comply with the authority, sixes fear retribution both from the authority and from what they have internalized of it, a strong and active superego. Of course, individual sixes may or may not rebel against their authority figures in later life, but the pattern of orienting themselves to life by obtaining the approval of others (who, in one way or another, function as authority figures) is one that has become ingrained in their nature.

Of all the personality types, sixes can be the most engaging and lovable people imaginable when they are healthy. The reactive quality of their psyches makes them delightfully playful and unpredictable. They want to be liked, and they have endearing, child-like qualities which we find in no other personality type. If they trust you, they can be the most loyal of friends. If you enjoy their loyalty, they will fight for you as they would for themselves-indeed, even better.

Average sixes, however, can be too dependent on the authority figure, while at the same time, reacting against their dependence and displaying the passive-aggressive ambivalence we have seen. When their aggressive side gets the upper hand, average sixes can be the most petty and mean-spirited of people—bigoted, authoritarian, and prejudiced—not at all lovable or endearing, as they were when they were healthy. And if they become unhealthy, sixes feel painfully insecure and extremely anxious, overreacting to everything as their wildly fluctuating emotions create severe problems for themselves and others. If they cannot resolve their anxieties and conflicts, sixes become self-defeating, bringing on themselves the very punishments they so fear.

Patterns in Malcom's life

To this point, we have purposely omitted Malcolm's surname. He had several, corresponding to the radical transformations he underwent during his lifetime. First, he was Malcolm Little, the son of Reverend Earl Little and Louise Little. Next, he was known as "Red" or "Detroit Red" in his days as a hustler on the streets of Boston and New York. In prison, he was known to some as 'Satan' because he was at war with God. After prison in Massachusetts, he took the name Malcolm X, the surname being the manner in which the Nation of Islam, his newfound religion, symbolized the true African family name that the black man never could know. The surname X would be carried by the church member" ... until God Himselfreturned and gave us a Holy Name from His own mouth." Finally, after his expulsion from the nation, and after his pilgrimage to Mecca, his name changed again, to El-Hajj Malik ElShabazz, the name he carried to his death in 1964, at age 40.

Malcom Little

As a result of their childhood experiences, sixes identify positively with their fathers or a father figure. Malcolm Little's earliest recollection was of a hostile white world. Malcolm's father had been a dedicated organizer for Marcus Aurelius Garvey's UNIA (Universal Negro Improvement Association) in Omaha, Nebraska, and later in Milwaukee, and then Lansing, Michigan. Garvey and the UNIA, headquartered in New York City's Harlem, were exhorting the Negro masses to return to their ancestral African homeland. The local Lansing hate group, the Black Legion, didn't like Reverend Little's preaching, and sent a terror squad to the Little home. With his eight children and pregnant wife inside, the terrorists set fire to Reverend Little's home. The family got out in time, but the house burned to the ground while white firefighters and police officers looked.

Reverend Earl Little moved his family to East Lansing, where he built a four-room house with his own hands. It was in this house that Malcolm grew up, exhibiting a strong connection to his father. Malcolm attended Baptist services where his father preached, and—according to his autobiographical account on page 199—he would sit "...goggle-eyed at my father jumping and shouting as he preached, with the congregation jumping and shouting behind him." Malcolm remembered especially his father's favorite sermon, on page four of his autobiography: " ... that little black train is a-comin' ... and you better get all your business right!" In later life, Malcolm would exhibit his father's ability to move an audience, and would preach a similar message.

Malcolm was six years old when his father was murdered. One is moved by the devastating effect this must have had on the boy as a human being. What of the murder's effect on Malcolm's psychological and emotional development? James W. Fowler offers this, in his essay titled, "The Pilgrimage in Faith of Malcolm X," found on page 40 of Trajectories of Faith: Five Life Stories:

"The energizing myth of a coming black rule in Africa, and of a realizable black manhood in America, must have taken on added sharpness because of the father's death ... Malcolm must have nurtured them and kept them burning like a hidden bull's-eye lantern within."

Here, then is the beginning of Malcolm's development: a young boy of six, who had heard a promise of hope from his own father whom he trusted, and who is subsequently murdered for his beliefs. Permanently etched on the young boy's memory is the importance of the father, and the father's message.

Sixes learn to follow the rules of the home and to become responsible members of society by being obedient, approved members of their first group, their families.

From here, Malcolm's world is turned upside-down. The struggle of his poor mother to keep food on the table, the unrelenting encroachment of the welfare authorities seeking to break the family apart, and the unresolved question of his father's death all worked upon Malcolm. His fulfillment in family became impossible, and he sought other sources for the fulfillment left by his father's absence, first in the home of neighbors (the Gohannas). Malcolm had become a behavior problem by this time, however, under the intense strain of his young life, and was sent to the home of the Swerlin family, in Mason, Michigan, the last stop before reform school.

Of all the personality types, sixes can be the most engaging and lovable people imaginable when they are healthy. It was at the Swerlins' home that Malcolm made the first of his remarkable "transformations." Brought there after various mischievous acts, Malcolm endeared himself to this family, was accepted, and welcomed in. Malcolm enrolled in Mason Junior High School, at the age of thirteen, where he excelled as a student. He was elected president of his seventh-grade class, and rose to the top of his eighth-grade class, competing for top honors with a white girl and boy.

Nothing in Malcolm's previous life following the death of his father predicted such a transformation. One can only say that it must have been a personality trait that made this possible. Malcolm needed to show that he could, if he wanted to, act like a responsible member of a family unit. All that was required was a will to do it, and Malcolm found that will. What happened to upset the balance he had found at the Swerlin home in Mason? Fowler again offers an explanation, based on Malcolm's account on page 36 of *The Pilgrimage in Faith of Malcolm X*:

> *"Looking back later, Malcolm recalls a symbolic conversation with a white eighth-grade teacher, a man who had seemed to like him, and who fancied himself an adviser to his students:*
>
> *He told me, 'Malcolm, you ought to be thinking about a career. Have you been giving it thought?' The truth is, I hadn't. I never have figured out why I told him, 'Well, yes, sir, I've been thinking I'd like to be a lawyer ... '*
>
> *Mr. Ostrowski looked surprised, I remember, and leaned back in his chair and clasped his bands behind his head. He kind of half-smiled and said,*
>
> *'Malcolm, one of life's needs is for us to be realistic. Don't misunderstand me now. We all like you here, you know that. But you've got to be realistic about being a nigger. A lawyer—that's no realistic goal for a nigger ..."*

Fowler concludes, "Malcolm came face to face with the fact that there was no sponsorship in Mason, religious or otherwise, for his giftedness and self-conscious blackness. The only conventional faith or identity white America seemed ready to offer him was a choice between sterile, whitewashed mediocrity and the demanding, ultimately selfdestructive negative identity of a borderline criminal" (*The Pilgrimage in Faith of Malcolm X*, pg. 49).

Malcolm ultimately rejected the familial place offered to him at the Swerlins, because his place was conditional; he had to be content as a "mascot," smart token Negro without ambition, or he wasn't welcome. Some choice! Malcolm left the Swerlins to live with his sister Ella, a proud black woman ("jet black" in Malcolm's words) who offered a hope of identity for the Negro boy. In Boston Malcolm made another of his startling transformations.

Detroit Red

Sixes are reactive, fluttering from one state to another very quickly. With a relocation to Boston, Malcolm transformed himself. He was thrilled with the pulse of the city, with the lights and sounds, and the action. What he mostly felt though was liberation, because he was now surrounded with black people, and a distinctly black culture. It was so far from the stifling existence as a "mascot" in the all-white junior high school in Michigan! Malcolm discovered a culture in which love and respect were unconditional, in sharp contrast to the conditions imposed on him in Lansing.

There were limited legitimate employment opportunities in 1940 for an African-American boy who had the drive and ambition of Malcolm. Given this, it wasn't surprising that Malcolm found his way into the world of illegitimate business. There were pockets of prosperity, to be sure in Roxbury in 1940. The borough received significant 'foreign exchange' from the surrounding white towns, whose men and women clandestinely came to revel in the speakeasies and joints of Roxbury's entertainment trade. Much of the trade was illicit. The Roxbury community had, by this time found a lucrative 'niche' in all of those activities of commerce that were outlawed: alcohol (during Prohibition), drugs, prostitution, gambling, and the numbers rackets. These were the "hustles," as Malcolm called them, and to the hustles Malcolm gravitated.

If sixes trust you, they can be the most loyal of friends. If you enjoy their loyalty, they will fight for you as they would for themselvesindeed, even better.

Malcolm began to form friendships immediately. His first and closest friend was a musician named "Shorty" who showed Malcolm the hustling world. Malcolm shined shoes at the Roseland Ballroom, in the course of which he started selling reefers-marijuana cigarettes. He went on to a variety of other hustles, making himself a fixture in the Roxbury underworld;

he was barely fifteen.

Another fast friend of Malcolm's was Sophia, a white woman who loved Malcolm for many years, and who wound up going to prison after becoming involved in Malcolm's burglary activity. Malcolm eventually broke apart from his sister Ella, who did not approve of the lifestyle into which he was sinking, and drifted down to New York City's Harlem, where he continued deeper and deeper into the world of drugs, narcotics, and other hustles. In time, Malcolm was run out of town, winding up back in Boston where he became a burglar.

Sixes are full of contradictions: they are emotionally dependent on others, yet do not reveal much of themselves. Sixes feel painfully insecure and extremely anxious, overreacting to everything as their wildly fluctuating emotions create severe problems for themselves and others. If they cannot resolve their anxieties and conflicts, sixes become self-defeating, bringing on themselves the very punishments they so fear.

During his time as a hustler, Malcolm became increasingly paranoid. Having crossed a big-time hustler named West Indian Archie, Malcolm began carrying not one, but two, and sometimes three guns. He trusted no one. This mistrust carried over into his life later on, as exemplified in his remark to the writer Alex Haley, who edited his autobiography, found on page 383: "You're another of the white man's tools sent to spy!" and on page 389 "I don't completely trust anyone. Not even myself. I have seen too many men destroy themselves ... you, I trust about twenty-five percent."

Just before he was caught by the police, Malcolm exhibited self-defeating behavior at least twice, bringing on his own downfall. First, he addressed his friend Sophia in a familiar way at a very indiscreet moment, risking discovery of their liaison by her family. And then he got himself caught by the police, bringing a very expensive watch he had stolen to a legitimate jeweler for repair! Nabbed, "Detroit Red" found himself in prison. At this point, he underwent a third transformation.

"Satan"

Sixes are likable and endearing, yet can be mean and hateful. In prison, Malcolm was forced to turn inwards. All of his multiple outside stimulants—drugs, sex, money, gambling, illicit business and huge profits—were now gone. Malcolm was left to confront himself. In prison, Malcolm met men who had found redemption by looking within ... but not Malcolm—at least not at first. He was barely twenty-one when he landed in Charlestown prison in 1946, and he was not prepared for religious conversion, and wanted no part of any talk of God, Allah, religious rituals, or any of that. He wanted out.

In prison, he was known as "Satan" among some of the inmates for his profanity, anger, and apostasy. With guidance from his lifelong sibling and brother Reginald (separated by less than two years from Malcolm), Malcolm eventually began a conversion to the Muslim faith as taught through the Nation of Islam. Another transformation, Malcolm's fourth had commenced. This transformation was radical, a "ricochet," in Enneagram terms, in the opposite direction from "Satan."

Malcom X: Life in Prison

According to his autobiographical account to Haley, Malcolm began to read in prison.

> *"A prisoner has time that he can put to good use. I'd put prison second to college as the best place for a man to go if he needs to do some thinking. If he's motivated in prison, he can change his life"* (The Autobiography of Malcolm X pg 389).

Transferred to the Norfolk Correction facility m Massachusetts, which had a liberal self-improvement program, and an extensive library donated by a man named Parkhurst, Malcolm began a program of selfeducation, mostly in history. About the Parkhurst collection, Malcolm would say later: "Any college library would have been lucky to get that collection" (*The Autobiography of Malcolm X* pg. 173). Malcolm now began an intensive study of the principles of the Nation ofIslam, with all of the considerable energy and ambition at his disposal. He also began a daily correspondence with Elijah Muhammad, the church's central figure, known as "the Messenger."

As they grow up, their positive identification with their fathers shifts to an identification with more abstract father figures, such as civil authorities or belief systems from which they can obtain security.

It is at this point in Malcolm's life that we point to the strongest evidence of his being a six in the Enneagram system—the Loyalist. What is so striking about Malcolm's conversion in prison is his complete, uncritical acceptance of the nation's catechism.

This lack of skepticism is uncharacteristic of "Malcolm the hustler," who trusted no one, and saw the world as a hustle. We can only conclude that there was some personality trait that made this acceptance possible, and the Enneagram may help give some insight into what this trait was.

Malcolm as a six provides a very good explanation of the personality trait that made such a total, breathtakingly immediate acceptance of the Nation of Islam and its doctrines possible. As we have seen, transformation was nothing new for Malcolm: He had exhibited the tendency before. What is different in this case though is the blindness of the loyalty offered up to Elijah Muhammad without reservation, and without all the information. Malcolm says so later, on pages 365 and 429 of his autobiographical account.

"There, on a holy world hilltop, I realized how very dangerous it is for people to hold any human being in such esteem, especially to consider anyone some sort of 'divinely guided' and 'protected' person ... I was a zombie then-like all Muslims-I was hypnotized, pointed in a certain direction and told to march."

How could a rational (he was no longer on drugs), intelligent (he read voraciously and retained what he read), cagey (he survived "like a ferret" for years on the streets) man like Malcolm fail to see many partial truths, (even a bit of the hustle) in Nation of Islam teaching, scattered throughout his autobiography? For example:

- Wallace D. Fard as God in person? (The Autobiography of MalcolmX, pg. 161)
- That his being in prison wasn't at least partially (mostly) his own choice? (pg. 169)
- That his first impression on hearing that white men were devils was of Hymie, (A Jew!) whom he remembered as a true friend? (pg. 159)
- That he had been looking forward to "the hype" that his brother Reginald was bringing to get him out of jail ... and religion was it! (pg. 158)
- That setting up some antagonist (whites) as the devil incarnate is the almost-oldest hustle in the world?

Malcolm's blinders are puzzling, but not inexplicable; the Enneagram seems to explain his uncritical acceptance. As a six, he was predisposed to such an allegiance, and, under the serious stresses and strains of his traumatic childhood and (later on) dissolute lifestyle and ultimate nadir in prison, he could do no less than to grab onto something to stop his slide.

Especially a doctrine that explained his own condition in such simplistic terms, shifting virtually all personal responsibility onto whites and Jews.

When their aggressive side gets the upper hand, average sixes can be the most petty and mean-spirited of people—bigoted, authoritarian, and prejudiced—not at all lovable or endearing, as they were when they were healthy.

Following his release from prison, Malcolm began his professional career, first as a missionary for the nation, then as its most eloquent spokesman. He became a social critic as well, frightening white audiences with his talk of "white devils," "rapist slave masters," etc. He was neither lovable nor endearing during this very aggressive period. Malcolm was angry at segregation and at the thousand-and-one indignities that colored people were subjected to every day, designed to remind them of their second-class citizenship, and vented the anger to his audiences. Malcolm's anger was real.

During this period trouble started to develop between Malcolm and Elijah Muhammad. In his zeal to preach the message, Malcolm may have been using Nation of Islam doctrine in a way in which it wasn't meant to be used, antagonizing Elijah Muhammad, "the Messenger." Malcolm had been advised, for instance by Elijah Muhammad to stay off college campuses, not a primary target for the nation's message.

However, Malcolm couldn't resist these engagements and became a visible, national figure, which Elijah Muhammad did not necessarily want. Nor did he feel completely comfortable with Malcolm's growing national stature, particularly as the nation's message was now being distorted by a fearful national press. Malcolm had started to become a liability for the nation.

They worship authority, yet fear it ... It is important to point out that Malcolm did indeed worship Elijah Muhammad, as he recounts in his autobiography penned by Haley, on page 306: " ... I actually had believed that if Mr. Muhammad was not God, then he surely stood next to God."

Given this blind loyalty, even adoration of another man, Malcolm had set himself up for the inevitable crisis when he was to learn that Elijah Muhammad was simply a man, just like himself after all. Elijah Muhammad had a bit of the hustler in him, just like Malcolm; he had had a woman on the side, just like Malcolm; and he had used Malcolm just like Malcolm had used countless others in his hustles. Confronting Elijah Mohammed's humanity meant that Malcolm had to confront his own. This brought on the fourth and final transformation in Malcolm's life.

El-Hajj Malik El-Shabazz: Enneagram Direction of Integration (the six goes to nine)

Near the end of his life, Malcolm began to achieve a truer sense of identity. The crisis brought on by his falling-out with the father figure Elijah Muhammad allowed him to see himself more as an individual, apart from the person with whom he had for so long identified himself It was liberating for Malcolm, as symbolized by his pilgrimage to Mecca in 1964. At Mecca, Malcolm was transformed again. The blinders he had worn for so long had fallen off, and he saw himself and the world in a completely different light. He found himself a member of the family of the Islamic faith, with no class, race or gender qualifications. White ate bread with black, and both worshipped the same Allah. As a symbol of this final transformation, Malcolm took the name El-Hajj Malik El-Shabazz.

In terms of the Enneagram and SoulScope®, we say that Malcolm had begun and was well along in the process of integration, or "transformation," a movement from one state to a higher stage of personal development. For the Six, the direction of integration is to Nine, the Peacemaker.

Sixes at Nine are quite different from even healthy Sixes. A revolutionary change for the better has taken place in the integrating Six: he becomes independent and yet, paradoxically, is closer to others than ever before.

By 1964, Malcolm had broken with the Nation of Islam. He was now independent, attempting to gather his personal followers into a new organization, the Organization of African-American Unity (OAAU). He was still energetic, working with a sense of urgency, but his attitude had changed somewhat, and his direction was changing as well. Indicative of this was that the national press confusion as to where he stood, and a resulting loss of interest in his cause. They stopped covering him as they had been.

Conclusion

As we stated earlier, Malcolm's personality was complex, not given over to smug classifications. It has been shown that Malcolm might be classified, despite these reservations, as a six in the Enneagram and SoulScope® systems, and that he was moving towards fulfillment in the six direction of integration—to the nine, or peacemaker.

It is unfortunate that his life was snuffed out prematurely, for he no doubt would have done even greater work in later years. He might have become involved in the civil rights movement in a central capacity, because of his unique attractiveness to inner-city black youth. Or he might have become a spokesman for an African nation or cause, such as the South African nationalist movement. Or perhaps his awakening to the needs of his native Africa may have placed him in an important diplomatic role. It is a great tragedy of American history that he should have died, at age forty so young, and when he had finally begun to realize a bit ofliberation and self-awareness after such a hard, hard life.

And as Andrew Young has so well stated, Malcolm would no doubt have been a major influence on urban youth, who so much needed the most authentic model of some one who had been to hell, and back, and was now leading others to higher ground.

Malcolm can be said to have maximized his soul through engagement and struggle with the realities and forces of his era, which are alive and well at the mid-point of this new decade of the 21st century, and millennium. Understanding his SoulPrint gives us a rich resource for people of faith who seek to firm up a new future, with and for the millions of especially young men, Amafrican and Hispanic, who languish in prison, or are headed there right now, and for generations to come, unless present trends are reversed. This is indeed a major part of the legend, legacy, and soul print of "our shining prince," a powerful exemplar, as Ossie Davis would refer to Malcolm in the memorable eulogy delivered by his friend.

Chapter 7

Restoration Jubilee: Setting the Captives Free

From the praise house, to the jailhouse, and back.

Setting the captives free is a jubilee requirement that calls out to workers and leaders in community and faith-based institutions and their allies in governmental, educational, corporate, criminal justice, and philanthropic sectors.

When Amafricans ask if there is a vision and a plan, which can essentially rescue and deliver us, and in the process make all Americans benefit, we will get some different answers than ever before.

After more than 50 years of personal apprenticeship in black church leadership (ordained 50 years); serious scholarship (over 40 years in formal study); and hopeful leadership in community economic and spiritual development I, Brother Virgil, being mindful of all I have been taught by personal and social history, do declare today, that there is such a vision and such a plan.

The overall plan is based on the undying wisdom of our African slave forebears, coupled with the central justice program put forward by the Bible, called jubilee, known mainly for its absence from the history of Christendom. It was by the former that our foreparents within 40 years of the Emancipation Proclamation year, had built the foundational infrastructure of black churches, black families, black colleges, black land ownership, black press, and black businesses-by which we as a race have at least survived 'till now. It was by the latter, that they charted their course. A core component of jubilee is the injunction to "set the captives free." This writer—having had the privilege of originating The Jubilee Bible—published and available from the American Bible Society, with this calling card is now calling all who care, to its mandate.

The current part of the plan to which I refer calls for a jubilee-led consortium over the next seven to 10 years, to focus on a comprehensive program to reverse the Jail Trail, running throughout all poor communities, especially African American and Hispanic. I call this 10-year plan, Restoration Jubilee. There are many who think dialogue, plan, organize, and work seriously at inner city economic development and healing. At this point, among the many factors which they must discuss, research, understand, and manipulate to that end, is that one often neglected, critical-path factor of "what's happening along the economic pathway between the ghetto house and the jailhouse." We must reverse the Jail Trail on the back end, prevent its necessity on the front end, and redeem it in the middle.

This is an unabashed appeal to jubilee, faith-inspired and community leaders and organizations to rise to this momentous challenge, and join with other necessary and willing allies in this major effort to restore persons, families, economies, communities and societies.

If the incarceration of so many African-American and Hispanic citizens represents the new slavery, then the reentry and the return of over 600,000 said persons to our communities across America, represents the new reconstruction or restoration. With more than 70% of those returnees going back to prison, that high recidivism rate indicates that the new reconstruction is our biggest failure at this point, but also our biggest challenge.

To that end, many community groups are coming together in states all across America, to galvanize the will, the strategies, and the collaboration necessary to a successful movement of reentry, return, and restoration of persons, families, communities, economies, and societies.

The Jubilee national Fellowship

Thus, a network was launched at Lynchburg, Virginia, in July 2002, called Jubilee National Fellowship. An account of its activities, witness to history, is attached. The coalition, led by several faith-inspired entities, includes some highly successful models of reentry and prevention, as well as models during incarceration bringing about wholesale transformation of inmates during incarceration, notably the work at the Santa Clara County Jail, under the tutelage of the Health Realization Institute. It represents the most thorough and lasting results in inmate transformation to be found in the country. The Health Realization movement is emerging in many places across this land, and is even having dramatic results in prisons in South Africa.

The Health Realization Institute: Been There, Done That!

Following the national attention paid to the highly successful outcomes of the Modello-Homestead Gardens project in Dade County, Florida, the Health Realization Institute (formerly RC. Mils & Associates) was asked to develop a training model for the comprehensive community revitalization project in the South Bronx. This year and a half long "training of trainers" program gave an opportunity to pilot a Health Realization training of trainers' model for staff and resident leadership of six large community development corporations. These corporations were a part of the revitalization project, which ultimately provided social services, community development, empowerment, economic development, employment, healthcare and mental health services to a catchment area of 250,000 residents.

After this project was completed, in 1994, we were asked to develop an ongoing program for Santa Clara County, to train and certify Health Realization teachers for countywide implementation of Health Realization personal and community empowerment programs. The training program in Santa Clara County has now been in operation for seven years, and has culminated in the training of over 2,000 practitioners in the jails, welfare to work, drug prevention and treatment, family violence, youth programs, social services, probation, and homeless programs.

Results produced in the large county jail at Santa Clara show the effectiveness of Health Realization in transforming inmates while incarcerated with dramatic and long lasting change once they return to the communities from which them came originally, what the coalition would call "redeeming the Jail Trail in the middle."

Perhaps the best-known and proven model for reentry and reversing the back end of the Jail Trail is the highly acclaimed Glidepath to Recovery, led by Father Peter Young of Albany, New York. It represents the solid core of a model of the future community that works. Glidepath to Recovery is part of the coalition's model for replication across the country, in constellation with the one church, ten-family model. The New Canaan International Church of Richmond, Virginia, is one of five churches developing this model as part of the Children's Defense Fund campaign to "Leave No Child Behind." A thumbnail sketch of both models follows.

Glidepath to Recovery (Reversing the Jail Trail)

Peter Young Housing Industries and Treatment, under the direction of Rev. Peter G. Young, operates inpatient and outpatient residential facilities and counseling and evaluation programs, which provide programs of treatment and rehabilitation daily for more than 3,000 persons afflicted with the illness of alcoholism and substance abuse. It provides a housing and vocational component for the return of the ex-offenders to the community as part of a pre-release planning process. The system developed by Young, referred to as Glidepath to Recovery, provides an alternative, an environment where fellow addicts can work toward similar goals of abstinence, employment and self-determination.

The goal is to help ease the transition from incarcerated status to supervised civilian life. The program assists individuals in innovative and effective ways to confront and possibly overcome the underlying problems that trigger and sustain substance abuse, negative, and self-destructive, addictive behavior. The program provides the tools necessary for an individual to become self-empowered to enter society.

Attention to program effectiveness has produced a four-year, post-graduate recidivism rate of less than 10% for alcohol/substance abuse treatment program graduates who completed our programs between 1988-1992-the period for which a research study was completedcompared to 69% for the national average, including medium A- and Bsecurity classification. The incarcerated population is the fastest growing population today and, therefore, it is imperative that measures be taken immediately to curtail this growth.

The target population presents an array of common conditions and exhibits multiple problems: most have a background of poverty and educational disadvantage. They frequently have dropped out of school and have a history of engaging in anti-social, criminal, and selfdestructive behaviors. Their motivation, in the traditional middle-class definition, is often misdirected or totally lacking.

Their personal histories frequently show little evidence of successful adjustment to life due to the effects of post-incarceration syndrome. They need help with a complex array of problems so that they can take full advantage of any treatment, vocational, and employment opportunities. On the other hand, these individuals frequently possess strengths, which are often overlooked. Due to the multiple barriers faced by this population, it is difficult for them to access services and obtain the social service reimbursement necessary to access treatment.

Rev. Young's facility is seeking funds for the enhancement of the existing programs and for replication of this model into other venues, and anticipates being able to both strengthen what they have going, and make their model available to other areas of the country.

The Front End of the Jail Trail: Prevention

In addressing the front end of the Jail Trail, we are primarily concerned with preventing our youth from having contact with the juvenile justice system; reducing the number of children who come under the control of the social service system through foster care; and reversing the lack of adequate education in our public school system. All of these factors propel the youth of poor and inner city communities along the path to the Jail Trail through juvenile jail, and ultimately, to adult incarceration.

One program that addressed these issues is "One Church, Ten Families." The program is a signature project of the Juvenile and Family Court Judges' Leadership Council of the Children's Defense Fund, based in Washington, DC. The council is a national network of more than 150, African-American juvenile and family court judges. Their mission is to formulate community-based prevention programs designed to reduce the number of children referred for court intervention, to encourage the replication of a wide range of positive juvenile justice practices, and to implement programs to prevent recidivism.

To this end, the leadership council launched pilot programs in five cities in 1999: Washington, DC; Baltimore, MD; Detroit, MI; Houston, TX; and Richmond, VA. Under this pilot program, juvenile and family court judges-when appropriate-refer youth offenders to a non-profit arm of a church participating in the "One Church, Ten Families" program.

In the Richmond program, they have trained and certified mentors (12 hours of classroom training required) who embrace the youth and his/her family with mentoring and supportive services. Additionally, the youth participate in an after school (afternoon program in summer) program comprised of academic enhancement, computer skills development and behavioral management. These youth are assigned for a period of six months and if they successfully complete the program, they will have no juvenile record. Successful completion of the program constitutes the development and beginning implementation of a life plan and demonstrated positive adjustment in behavior.

Many traditional sentencing diversion programs can be characterized as band-aid rehabilitation approaches. Many programs merely monitor the progress and behavior of the youth's environment. However, research has demonstrated that there are multiple determinants to adolescent criminal behavior. The social system of family, peers, school, and community are directly related to antisocial behavior. These social systems, each of which is intertwined with a young person's development are integral elements of prevention, rehabilitation, and family restoration efforts. The solution is a comprehensive program that addressed all of a youth's social systems.

The youth and family restoration approach recognizes the significant role of religious institutions in the development of the family. This particular model provides three strategies with interventions for each: the youth prevention strategy, family/caregiver focused strategy, and the church intervention strategy.

The youth prevention strategy includes mentoring, life skill enhancement, job training and career development, academic enrichment, peer networking, and mental health interventions. The family/caregiver focused strategy includes community resource sharing, parent/caregiver networking, and parental mentoring interventions. The church intervention strategy includes the installation of hope and reinforcing values, and juvenile justice and family court advocacy.

Research shows that children fare better when there is at least one caring adult involved and that this type of intervention is best accomplished early on. And so, the "One Church, Ten Families" programs contain a prevention component designed to deter younger siblings from delinquency while building stronger families. Increased parental involvement is essential in achieving lower recidivism. Moreover, by providing troubled youth and their families a caring network of concerned community members, this program intends to both strengthen families and reverse the front end of the Jail Trail.

The coalition believes that by bringing together in the affected communities, operations representing the three points along the continuum of the Jail Trail, we will have created the single most critical the factor which most highly predicts success for the reentry, return, and restoration effort.

Other Considerations

Several major pre-conditioning factors can now be set forth. First, is what one might call the ghetto house, as a symbol of all that's happening and not happening in the home community institutions, which make today's prison inmate what he is. He is mainly young, black and/or Hispanic, illiterate, and poor. Furthermore, he is a victim of the economically deprived environment foisted upon him, his family, and his community. But he might be encouraged like the new Malcolm X, to go from victim to victor.

The second factor-which can no longer be overlooked-in deciding strategies for the economic development and healing of inner city communities, families, and persons, is the devastating impact of the jailhouse itself, and all that it encompasses and symbolizes. It is the death of hope for inner city youth. The jailhouse stands as the symbol of our society's almost total surrender to racism, and all the negative forces it has in large part, mainly helped create. It has—in the considered opinion of serious commentators on the subject—become the new slavery.

The third pre-conditioning factor which must be taken into account in this equation is that of the public till, and its governmental authorities which appear to be stumbling blindly in the wasteful spending of tax dollars in such a way as appears to mainly cause the problem to get worse. At an average cost of $40,000 plus, and rising; our brothers and sisters are being warehoused and made worse, not better. In Rhode Island, the cost for incarcerating juvenile offenders is over $100,000 per year. And the total tax bill is rising, and its end is not in sight. In addition to being good for the local communities, such a plan would plug up a sinkhole of good dollars being thrown away chasing bad social policy, solving nothing, and in the process making things worse all around.

Restoration: Jubilee Role Models

Jailhouse Jubilee is inspired equally by the lives and teachings of King, Malcolm X, and Nelson Mandela. Dr. King led many of us off to jail in the civil rights movement, and in the process and during those demonstrations, two quite significant things happened. One, crime in those inner communities themselves dropped to near zero. And, secondly, during our times in prison, the hymns, freedom songs, prayers, bible readings, and study sessions the demonstrators had with those already there when we got there, temporarily transformed those jail houses from "dungeons of shame, into houses of hope." Life inside the jails didn't phase or daze us; it was a deep challenge, creatively met. And we can meet it again.

Malcolm X went into the prison as victim and self-confessed hustler, and illiterate. He emerged a leader, and he became a healer. But in the process, he had to invent his own way of educating himself while in jail, and making himself, and a great many others marketable from that transformation. What Malcolm X stumbled on within the prison walls, we can and we must now routinize and institutionalize through Restoration Jubilee.

For those persons behind bars, these prisons must become major centers of learning, healing, earning and owning, and we will have bought for ourselves a new future, and especially for their families and communities. Above all, for the whole country, which by this process, can be well on the way towards its own healing, where racism and poverty are giving way to the open and affluent society, the true beginnings of our Beloved Community, USA.

Now, the critical question: Is there a viable institutional candidate on the national scene, which has what it takes to get us all together to make this happen? The other critical question to be addressed, is: What is needed in an institutional partnership for the prevention, redemption, and reversal of the Jail Trail, and the restoration of persons, families, communities, and societies to nobility, productivity, civility and viability?

The institutions necessary to this partnership include faith-inspired, governmental, educational, corporate, criminal justice, philanthropic, and community sectors.

The answer to the first question is yes, the black church, energized into what our African forebearers called the pray's house, could get us to first base. Beyond that, the black church-collectivized, focused, and intentional about implementing such a master plan for rescue and deliverance could catalyze all the forces and resources of the entire black community and the entire nation, and all our progressive minded allies who desire to see a new American future in black and white and all other colors.

Traditionally, this slavery predicament has been a black and white issue in America. But now, America has become a nation with all the colors of God's human family, and persons and communities, mainly poor, are in the soup together. We must fashion and implement solutions together. Thus the work of Restoration Jubilee is a call to persons, families, institutions, and communities in black and white, and all other colors, for we have the opportunity and challenge, to reverse not only the Jail Trail, but to become pathfinders together, in walking and working together, blazing new trails towards our common Beloved Community for which King lived and died, and for which jubilee allies continue to strive.

Next, Dr. Judy Sedgeman offers her perspective on the program, in a report she prepared for the Sydney Banks Institute newsletter.

Witnessing History
by Judy Sedgeman

Last week, I was part of a meeting that will become an historic turning point in the annals of hope for all people, regardless of their circumstances, and of service to the "poorest" among us.

To look at the very attendance roster for this gathering, never mind the agenda of events, would be to see impossibility and judge it unlikely to succeed. Indeed, the hopefulness of the event is illuminated by its improbabilities and the fact that it succeeded anyway, creating visible proof that circumstances have nothing to do with the possibility of transcending them.

The primary organizers of this event were two men who would be presumed to have nothing in common: Dr. Virgil Wood, a Harvard educated, African-American man, who spent the first 10 years of his career as a member of Dr. King's inner circle, organizing campaigns for civil rights; and Dr. Jerry Falwell, an evangelist who stood firmly on the other side of the civil rights movement 40 years ago and who once had a reputation for distaste for all minorities. Indeed, Dr. Wood and Dr. Falwell described themselves, with considerable light-hearted irony, as "the odd couple" but spoke of their current friendship and common vision for positive change in ways that genuinely resolved the differences of the past with forgiveness and respect.

On Thursday evening, July 12, 2001, these two men stood side by side behind the pulpit of the Court Street Baptist Church, a beautiful landmark building in Lynchburg, Virginia, as the oldest AfricanAmerican church there, and talked about their shared vision for salvaging the lives of one of the least-loved, most feared and most costly segments of the American population: criminal recidivists who appear to be beyond rehabilitation.

I came to be there because curiosity became passion for positive change in the mind of Virgil Wood, who has never abandoned his faith that Martin Luther King's dream of freedom, dignity and equality for all people would be realized somehow, some day. For years, he has tirelessly sought out other people and programs that support the dream.

Only months ago, Virgil Wood heard that there was something happening at West Virginia University, where there was an Institute dedicated to research, education and service based on a simple paradigm for improving the quality of life for all people, regardless of circumstances. He came on his own to the first national conference sponsored by The Sydney Banks Institute for Innate Health, "Releasing the Power in Health," in Pittsburgh in mid-June, to see whether there was anything to this work. I encountered him the first night, as he was creating a program within the program for himself, trying to be sure to meet and interview as many people involved in the theoretical and practical aspects of "innate health" as he could. His intent was to investigate it thoroughly because the principle-based approach did, on first glance, seem too simple to be good and too good to be true. And like everyone else, he wondered why, if it was so effective, he had never heard of it, and he wondered if it was just another re-packaging of old methods with a new name.

During the days of the conference, he was up early and late; pulling people aside; asking probing questions; talking in depth to clients of the work as well as practitioners who were there; gathering e-mail addresses, phone numbers, program information from all over the country. Within days, he was on the phone, announcing that he would be coming to West Virginia to make videotapes of the principals in the Sydney Banks Institute for Innate Health-including Dr. William Pettit, a psychiatrist who has based his practice on innate health for nearly 20 years and who is a medical consultant to the institute-and Sydney Banks, who was visiting at the time. From here, Dr. Wood was on his way to California, to videotape work being done there with substance abusers, jail inmates, perpetrators of violence, the homeless, substandard housing projects, community policing. And that was only the beginning of his research.

Within a three-month period, Dr. Virgil Wood traveled far, met many people, read many books and papers, and gathered sufficient evidence to feel confident that he was in touch with something he had longed to find ever since his youth with Martin Luther King. But most importantly, his own life had changed. As he opened his mind and heart to understanding what innate health is really pointing towards and to unravel its potential and implications, he had insights that changed his own experience of stress dramatically and he found himself operating at levels of creativity and productivity that even he found amazing. He was definitely no slouch in those areas in the first place. The changes he could see and feel within himself provided a deep foundation for his certainty that the changes he was observing in others were real and sustained.

Dr. Wood is pastor of the Pond Street Baptist Church of Providence, Rhode Island. Dr. Falwell is senior pastor of the Thomas Roads Baptist Church in Lynchburg, and is chancellor and founder of Liberty University. Together they had organized the Lynchburg conference called "Restoration Jubilee: Setting the Captives Free," with the goal of establishing "a dynamic working coalition for the successful re-entry of inmates into their communities, and the prevention of the Jail Trail on the front end-and in the process, to jump-start the community's economy."

Their intent was to brainstorm ways in which this could be accomplished and to look at programs that work. Their common ground was agreement that this was a cause that demands church leadership since churches are the community institutions set up to embrace and forgive and rehabilitate. They also agreed that whatever the mainstream efforts are that focus now on prisoner rehabilitation, they don't seem to be reducing recidivism or preventing people from entering what Dr. Wood calls the "Jail Trail," a cycle of hopelessness and insecurity that leads people into a lifetime of crime and self-loathing.

The church leaders they gathered to create this conference adopted a stance of open-minded consideration for any and all ideas that offered hope of attaining their goal. They agreed not to judge people or programs by their doctrine or beliefs, but rather by their spirit, and by their results. The

Lynchburg Program launched a national initiative that will sweep through many cities in the coming months, and create a huge coalition of people committed to creating an entirely different climate of hope for an end to violence, abuse, and the desecration of human dignity in this country.

So it was, that one month after meeting Virgil Wood, I sat in a spellbound audience at the Court Street Baptist Church as he talked about his understanding of mind, consciousness and thought and the discovery that he had made, at last, of a way that really works to reach the most disaffected people. Therefore, it was that, as he described "an extraordinary secular understanding now being taught so that the seeds of a miracle in wellness and prevention have been sown at West Virginia University Medical School," he asked me to stand to represent that miracle and the thousands of colleagues who have brought it to life throughout the world. So it was that a black and white checkerboard audience of ministers, social workers, psychologists, politicians, writers, doctors, parolees, retirees, teachers, counselors-people from all walks of life-shouted and cheered for the new hope for all people Dr. Wood had just laid out for them.

So it was that I was surrounded afterwards with people of all ages, races, creeds, asking for more information and asking what our university could offer them in terms of education or degrees in this promising work, and volunteering their service. And so it was considered "the poor." He said, "It does not mean observe or notice. It means to extend your compassion, to take into consideration, to include not exclude them." The next day, I was honored to speak to these people, assembled to consider next steps, and found myself borne far beyond my own loftiest hopes and dreams by the updrafts of their love and gratitude and enthusiasm.

Dr. Jerry Falwell talked about the poor as not just those with no means, but those who are spiritually bereft and alienated from others, wrapped up in their own fears and doubts. In considering the poor, he said, his church-all churches-should consider what works for people, what produces results. He concluded, "The difference between mediocrity and greatness is always vision."

Vision takes us beyond the known, to solutions we can imagine even if we do not yet see how to bring them to be. When we look to our vision, we enter a defining moment, a moment in which we can choose to be shaped by our dreams, not limited by our circumstances. The Sydney Banks Institute for Innate Health is as much a product of improbabilities as this meeting was. Improbabilities, unlikely happenings that are nonetheless true, are the gateways to discovery, the entry point of dreams.

The gathering July 12 and 13 in Lynchburg was a gathering of people who exemplify these words of Martin Luther King: "Love is the only force capable of transforming an enemy into a friend." They are excited at the prospect of building bridges with an institution, The Robert C. Byrd Health Sciences Center at West Virginia University, which has the courage to list "love" as an institutional value, the faith to embrace a new program that works on the strength of its results, and the integrity to put forth a vision for service to mankind beyond the known.

Judy Sedgeman, July 2001

Chapter 8

When America Buries Racism

Thanks to Senator Trent Lott, America can now (for the first time) really bury racism.

Senator Trent Lott should not be made the scapegoat for his remarks having the unintended, but salutary effect, of highlighting a nation that preaches equality but even now practices an ever more damaging form of racism. The racism of this period is a different type than that of the early part of the last century, but in its current more subtle, systemic form, is so virulent, that it has rendered any viable future for its black citizens even more problematic than it was during the mid sixties.

And Senator Robert Byrd's comment about "white niggers" needs to be seen as a similar blessing to the nation, an invitation for a serious exploration on how 'the mean-spirited treatment' of black poor people in America, impacts negatively, and is not unlike the treatment of all other poor people in America.

This racism may have had its most obvious manifestation in the South, but it is showing itself as much entrenched in the North and West as well as the South. For example, in Rhode Island, several examples come to mind, some current, and the others, ongoing.

First, the struggles within the Judicial Committee on disparities in sentencing by the courts, is just one example of a state community in search of its own soul, on this, and other critical issues.

A second and ongoing issue is the quiet refusal of Rhode Island's wealth holders who gained a significant economic advantage for their role as brokers in the slave trade, to become partners in a balanced exploration of reparations and restitution, as a legitimate task for the current appropriate parties, especially those deeply damaged by its ongoing residuals.

Senator Lott's ongoing leadership in the U.S. Senate was really over as soon as his historic remarks were out, but the legacy of racism continues unresolved. Congressman John Lewis reaching out to Trent Lott, in the same manner that Martin Luther King Sr. reached out to George Wallace and to Jimmy Carter, can have a like blessing for all. Daddy King embracing George Wallace made him one of the most compassionate political leaders later in his life. Daddy King embracing Jimmy Carter after his "ethnic cleansing statement," helped catapult Carter right into the White House. The reaching out blessed them, and saved their careers.

Perhaps now, Senator Lott and Congressman John Lewis can lead our nation in a requiem for racism. Yes, the nation has moved beyond the obvious atrocities of old style racism, and all that it now needs is a decent burial, and Senator Lott should be allowed a place at the head of the funeral march.

Nine months should be utilized in planning the funeral; after it is over, we can all get down to the business of lifting and launching the America of the Beloved Community and all working and benefiting from its new beloved economy.

This open invitation to the nation recognizes that reconciliation can only come when we all—black and white—agree to the funeral, and jointly sponsor it.

When America Does Bury Racism

When America buries racism, then black and white and all alike can have a good time and sing, "halleluiah, shalom, amen, and Asalamalakum."

With the virus of racism, undiagnosed, untreated, and un-buried the real life of our fellowship is shackled, deformed and destroyed ... until we bury racism.

When we bury racism, black folk will no longer have its long bony fingers of death intruding into every facet of their lives, ruling their thinking and ruining their being. Every fear that grows out of its crippling imprisonment will fly away like the birds of prey after we bury racism.

When we bury racism, it will be the undoing of the Willie Lynch curse and every evil promise will be drained of its compulsive power, and black Folk will at long last shed the corpse of their own fears, give up the hatred of our own black skins and the false love of our mulattoed predicament, and reclaim our humanity simply as the sons and daughters of Mother Africa and the children of father creator God. When we black folk give up racism!

When we give up racism, white folk-poor and rich alike, will at long last shed the guilt of unearned privilege and stolen legacies, come out of our long mid-night of denial, and we will seek an authentic membership in the family of humanity and the household of God. When we white folk give up racism!

When we give up the ghost of racism, black children will come out from under the evil cloud of an ascribed inferiority and a continuing imposition of educational contempt. These children will come to know who they really are and who their competent and caring ancestors arebuilders of pyramids and lovers of God and humanity ! After they and we, give it up!

When we all give up racism, it will no longer spread its tentacles of abuse, violence, crime and death, from the West to the East, from the North to the South. At that time, policemen will give up their bullets marked "for black not white." The mindset of hate in the KKK (among but not in all of the blue) will be exposed to the bright light of a cleansing high noon.

When America buries its racism, it will begin to reconcile its capital-producing power with the pitiful plight of its capital-less poor, and in the process, give to the world what Democracy promises, Jesus proclaims, and the Liberty Bell announces: "proclaim liberty throughout the land, unto all the inhabitants thereof."

When liberty is truly proclaimed throughout all the land and unto the uttermost parts of the earth, Africa will breathe free, the Middle East will find and enjoy peace, and Northern Ireland will find "the wind beneath their wings." And all God's children, as King continues to remind us, will overcome ... after we all bury racism!

We can and we will overcome the racism of contempt, low aim, and stolen legacies-and at long last put an end to the disease now encircling the earth through every outlet, whether through media or any other form of continuing colonial imposition. Let the very air we breathe become free of racism's pollution.

When the church and its institutional relatives give up racism, then Christ can come down from every cross, democracy can become the birth right of every nation, and abundance can become the birth mark of every land. Because we are giving up racism!

Giving racism a decent burial is in the interest ofus all. We therefore invite the whole family of humanity to begin planning the funeral march. And after we take the full nine months needed to plan the burial, we will be ready at long last, to stop off at the cemetery of catastrophe, bury this body of death in a well-marked grave, and then get on with our journey towards the Beloved Community and the kingdom of God. A requiem for racism is long overdue! Can't you hear the funeral dirge? What do you say? Isn't it time for beloved America to stand up?

Part Three:
Love Beyond Fear

"Calling the Four Winds" Ezekiel 37:9d

Chapter 9

Martin Luther King, Jr.: Why the Warrior was Peaceful

Often accused of fomenting conflict and strife, King was also recognized by the Nobel Peace Commission as the world leader in peace and non-violence. How can we reconcile these opposing viewpoints?

Introduction

Benjamin Elijah Mays is commonly thought of as an architect of King's notion of the Beloved Community and its manifest destiny, to heal the soul of America. In that assessment, Mays could be said to have established the African American and the dispossessed of America, firmly at second base in the American arena. King, as the American Gandhi, established the dispossessed community of America, as part of the Beloved Community firmly on third.

In 1957, King and other Ministers, mostly Southern, convened in New Orleans, and founded the Southern Christian Leadership Conference, which would become the Organization through which he would launch and carry out his movement to the end of his life.

In 1960, I was invited by Dr. King to join the Southern Christian Leadership Conference, and become a member of his national board, on which I would serve several years beyond his death.

When this leadership conference was founded in 1957, King and Rosa Parks had already become household names all across the nation. It would be 30 some years later, after my life-time involvement with civil rights and subsequent community development movements, that I would be privileged to have another earth-shaking experience, alike in depth, intensity, and impact, to my earlier involvement with King and the civil rights movement.

That came in 1991 when I was introduced to the Enneagram, and for an entire year, devoured every book on the subject I could find. At the end of that time, I took part in a weeklong training session of the Enneagram with Don Riso, and discovered to my utter amazement that those of us who shared the week in intensive study and involvement, perhaps knew each other in a way that few persons who knew us even longer, could fathom, or match. In my estimation, over the course of that week, I sensed that we had become a miniature Beloved Community.

The value of the Enneagram on my personal and family life, as well on my ministry and community work, is simply beyond measure. Having been part of Martin Luther King's "Dream Team" for over 10 years, searching and seeking for means of "building the Beloved Community" during the civil rights days, I am compelled to declare that for me, the Enneagram has to be set alongside Gandhi's Satyagraha theory and practice, adopted by King as a potent weapon in his movement.

Gandhi's approach gives us a reliable tool for growing society towards health and healing, while the Enneagram and SoulScope® make possible the same outcome in the inner lives of persons, the kind of people necessary to bring about King's version of the Beloved Community.

Historical Overview

For a brief introduction to the life of King, it will be helpful to sketch it out in brief, but useful fashion. The late James Washington, general editor of the anthology of King's writings and speeches, A Testament of Hope, renders the highlights, under his introduction, subtitled, "The Life of a Prophet."

The Life of a Prophet

Martin Luther King, Jr. was born in Atlanta, Georgia, on 15 January 1929. His parents were the Reverend King, Sr., and Mrs. Alberta Williams King. Between 1935 and 1944, he attended David T. Howard Elementary School,

Atlanta University Laboratory School, and Booker T. Washington High School. He passed a special examination to enter Morehouse College without finishing high school, and attended Morehouse between 1944 and 1948.

In the meantime, the Ebenezer Baptist Church in Atlanta, whose senior pastor was King's father, also licensed the son to preach, in 1947, when he was only 18 and ordained him to the Christian ministry on 25 February 1948. He graduated from Morehouse College with a bachelor's degree in sociology in June 1948. That September he entered Crozer Theological Seminary in Chester, Pennsylvania, a seminary affiliated with what was then called the Northern Baptist Convention (now called the American Baptist Churches in the USA). In 1951, he obtained his bachelor's degree in divinity at the head of his class. Encouraged by his seminary professors, he applied for the doctorate in systematic theology at Boston University School of Theology. He earned this degree within five years, and received it on 5 June 1955.

Within that five-year period, two events in his life were to be far more important than the doctorate in shaping his destiny. First, he married Coretta Scott of Marion, Alabama, on 18 June 1953. When they met in Boston, she was a recent graduate of Antioch College who was pursuing graduate study in singing at the New England Conservatory of Music.

Before he finished his dissertation, the historic Dexter A venue Baptist Church of Montgomery, Alabama, invited him to become their twentieth pastor. On 31 October 1954, amid much local fanfare, Martin and Coretta King were installed as the first family of this prestigious black Baptist church.

The second event took place on 1 December 1955. Mrs. Rosa Parks, a forty-two-year-old black seamstress, took an action that shook the racist South and signaled to African Americans that the time had come at last to unequivocally reply "No!" to racial segregation and discrimination. While riding the public bus from her job at the Montgomery Fair department store, this tired black worker was approached by a white man who boarded the bus and who remained standing rather than sit next to a black woman.

The bus driver demanded that she surrender her seat, as the Jim Crow laws of Alabama required. Rosa Parks said, "No." She was arrested. The fight to vindicate her ignited the civil rights movement of the 1960s. Her "no" became the indignant rallying cry for black people throughout America.

For 381 days, Dr. King, as president of the Montgomery Improvement Association, led a successful nonviolent black boycott against the Montgomery, Alabama, public bus system. In this boycott, the force of his personality and his deeply spiritual, intelligent preaching against violence and for justice made him an internationally know Christian proponent of nonviolent social change. He felt a decisive moment in history had arrived.

He declared, "after prayerful consideration I am convinced that the psychological moment has come when a concentrated drive against injustice can bring great tangible gains." King decided to institutionalize his newly acquired social power by founding the Southern Christian Leadership Conference in 1957. He resigned from his Montgomery parish in January 1960, and became the co-pastor of his father's church, Ebenezer Baptist Church, so that he could work full-time on his SCLC activities.

We could merely add here that Dr. King delivered (before the nationally-televised march on Washington on 28 August 1963) the historic keynote address we know as his "I Have a Dream" speech; that he received the 1964 Nobel Prize for Peace; and that he was assassinated in Memphis, Tennessee, on 4 April 1968. But such a terse narrative would not disclose the historical significance of the period between the publication of Dr. King's Stride Towards Freedom in 1958 and his death in 1968. In this brief span of time, the United States experienced a moral, religious, and political revolution whose tremors were felt around the world.

Martin Luther King: An Eight with a Nine Wing

Martin Luther King was a strong-willed individual. To those around him, his gift of leadership was tempered by a certain forcefulness in getting his own way. King not only saw his life as a struggle, but also had the courage to do something great, the surest mark of the eight. Of all the types of the Enneagram, eights are the most openly aggressive personalities. They are take-charge people who want to impose their wills on the environment, including, of course, other people. Because they are so strong-willed and forceful, eights are among the easiest types to identify, although for the same reason they are the most difficult to deal with because getting their way is so important to them. King clearly was an eight. It was his eight type that gave Martin Luther King his vision and his ability to stay the course. It helps account for his resourcefulness, and the fearlessness that accepts no challenge as being too tough. The Asserter will right a wrong without regard to their own personal position will carry the weak on their brave shoulders. The force of conviction, the drive to serve the un-served, and the independence of the Eight all helped Dr. King break the chains.

Yet King's forceful eight personality was tempered by a softer, more passive side. We shall argue that this was a function of his nine wing. The nine of the Enneagram is, like the eight, in the relating triad. Unlike the eight, however, the nine sees in his world harmony and peace, and attempts to maintain this equilibrium balance in all things, particularly in human relationships. To accomplish this, the nine can be self-effacing, accepting of conventional roles, easygoing, and accommodating to others.

The nine and eight are, in many respects, opposed. A great deal of conflict can erupt in nine-wing personality types. Whereas the eight vigorously presses his agenda in his world, the nine tends to be more accommodating towards others. While the nine looks towards inner peace, the eight tends to focus on concrete action. Reconciliation of the eight and nine traits can cause a great deal of confusion in nine wings, and more importantly mixed messages.

Dr. King seems to have found a balance between his eight and nine personality traits, as the following presentation will hopefully show. But that isn't all. King's relationship to his parents is developed in some depth, as is his relationship to the church and his early upbringing in it. The reader will see that the early years were important to King's development, probably more so than his years in formal educational study. He attempted to synthesize the ideas of religion, of politics, and of personal lifestyle. It is possible that the synthesis of forces in his own life was a reflection of King's deeper, inner attempts to synthesize conflicting eight and nine personality traits.

Dr. King was a man for his people, a man for his country, and a man for his world. In general, he found it necessary to put practical results over more abstract concepts, at least during the civil rights movement. His leadership ability was unquestioned, and he was known primarily for being practical-minded when it came to achieving concrete results.

Dr. King brilliantly gave people direction and motivation. He underscored the multilevel nature of community for the 21st century, translating how we are members of a national community, of an ethnic community, of a local community or communities, and a world community, all at the same time. He conveyed that the most culturally mature are able to live and feel at home, in the broadest level of community-the world. This was cultural pluralism at its best, and people saw King as a champion of these principles, for all people, and believed that he would use all of his many gifts to help them make something of themselves.

Dr. King had to spend a disproportionate amount of time and emphasis overcoming obstacles, both within his own community as well as beyond. His ability to do this, particularly in his later years was due in no small part to his own inner spirituality development. For even as he struggled to maintain coalitions within the civil rights movement, he was also wrestling with two conflicting sets of personality inclinations. He was a leader, but a philosopher; a political scientist but a prophet of peace; a motivator, but a deeply inner-directed person.

Particularly in the later years of the civil rights struggle (1965-68), King found it necessary to overcome increasing opposition and inertia. He was unable, for example, to adequately address the problems and prospects regarding the internal development of black America, or to focus the massive machinery of the civil rights movement on such internal development. It was only through his confidence and the strength of his personality that he was able to turn the growing movement in the direction he wanted to steer, namely towards economic justice and economic opportunity within the black community.

His ability to overcome obstacles was matched by his ability to take action. It was easy for him to assume leadership, because he had little problem making decisions. This is no more evident than during his years of action-oriented ministry, when King had to take on an entire nation, even though it gave him less time than he really needed to address the internal and developmental needs of the black community itself. This aspect was rooted in his eight personality: generally speaking, his actions were based on the needs of the situation.

It was well known that he took the initiative and didn't mind pushing to get what he wanted. At the outset of his work in Montgomery in 1955, for example, every level of black life in America and every circle was absolutely quiescent before the dehumanizing system that segregated and brutalized any and all, regardless of their socioeconomic situation or status. King shook the foundations of that system at every level in distinct reverberating waves, touching the black wealthy, whose independence was greatest (given their larger number of life chances and options), all the way over to the black jail class, whose life chances were about nil.

King's heart, mind, soul, and strength were focused on "how to keep my people aroused to positive action ... militant enough ... and moderate enough ... to keep it within Christian bounds," as he so eloquently stated in his book, *Stride Towards Freedom*. In his final speech on 3 April 1968, he carried the same message as in his non-violent inaugural speech at the Holt Street Baptist Church on the night of 5 December 1955: he wanted people to help themselves, and he would show them how. Indeed, "We as a people" was his concluding word and testament to the entire world. Helping others and leading the way was a distinguishing mark of Dr. King's character, indicating his strong eight personality.

Expressing frustration was rare for King, because he didn't want to reveal weakness, and rarely did. This was also understandable when King is viewed through the Enneagram description of an eight. As we have indicated, despite Dr. King's ability to act quickly, to get things done, near the end of his life he began to feel and express frustration for himself and the Movement, perhaps a result of the more-sensitive nine wing. Bill Adler, editor of *The Wisdom of Martin Luther King in His Own Words*, references one such occasion in 1961, where King succinctly states:

"We have become so involved in trying to wipe out the institution of segregation, which certainly is a major cause of social problems among Negroes that we have neglected to push programs to raise the moral and cultural climate in our Negro neighborhoods."

Without reading too much into quotes such as these, it is possible to argue that King was fatigued in his later years, with his public ministry taking too much from his private life of self-examination, which for a nine wing is crucial to balanced development. This makes the following statement by Don Richard Riso-taken from *Personality Types: Using the Enneagram for Self-Discovery*—truly applicable: "The inner sanctum [of the nine-wing subtype] is undisturbed and at peace, although it is doubtful that people of this subtype visit that inner part of themselves as much as they should. It remains an ideal" (pg 243).

Early Development

According to the address Professor Clayborne Carson presented at the Symposium on the History of African-American Christianity ("The Religious Evolution of Martin Luther King, Jr."), King scholars have not yet adequately explored the connections between King's personality development during his pre-adult years and his subsequent life as a political and religious leader. In his published writing, King said little about his childhood experiences and emphasized his graduate school training and readings as sources of his most important beliefs. The tendency of observers to depict him as the intellectual product of his academic training, his readings, or his acquaintance with Gandhian ideas misses the point: King was really a product of his early development and childhood origins, and his attachment to his father.

In his address, Carson further states that King himself described his childhood years as crucial to the development of his basic religious attitudes. He was rebellious towards established authority and tradition, as far as religion was concerned. He was more interested in synthesizing than in accepting established doctrine. As a leadership personality, this would be consistent. But his relationship with his father is most critical for a true understanding of King the man.

At least four generations of his ancestors had lived in the state of Georgia. His father was the Baptist minister of the Ebenezer Baptist Church in Atlanta, where King would eventually preach himself. But the stability of the King tradition in Atlanta is most noteworthy, because his grandfather and his maternal great-grandfather were also Baptist preachers. The King family was stable, to say the least, in the community, and King was fortunate to grow up in a fairly comfortable middle class environment. King's father was an activist minister and civil rights leader in his own right. He founded the Atlanta chapter of the NAACP, and undertook other activist preaching and ministerial functions. King looked up to his father for this reason.

King combined aspects of both his father's domineering will and the emotional nurturing of his mother. This would be the surest sign that King was an eight with a nine wing, but that topic will be discussed in detail below. King was questioning, but rarely challenged his father directly, preferring to wait until concrete conditions existed which would allow him to make his own statement. In 1950, he wrote:

> *"It is quite easy for me to think of a God of love mainly because I grew up in a family where love was central and where lovely relationships were ever present. It is quite easy for me to think of the universe as basically friendly mainly because of my uplifting hereditary and environmental circumstances. It is quite easy for me to lean more toward optimism than pessimism about human nature mainly because of my childhood experiences."*

The preceding quote-borrowed from King's "Autobiography of Religious Development"-clearly shows King's nine wing. The peacemaker side of King is illustrated sharply in this paragraph. The nine wing displays great equanimity and contentment ("the universe is friendly"). For the nine, the inner landscape is peaceful and contented. The whole picture, the entire situation is pleasant. More will be said about this below.

It was in his father's church that King learned to get along with people. In the very autobiographical document above, King states that among his peers and in Sunday School, he "... learned the capacity for getting along ..." This was probably due to his feeling at ease emotionally and psychologically in his environment, of which he was, because of his father, in a uniquely powerful position. As the child of the minister, the other children must have naturally deferred to him, which played to his eight's sense of control, and therefore of his sense of destiny.

The church was like a second home to King, the setting of his first important successes in childhood. When he was four, for example he received acclaim singing numbers such as "I Want To Be More and More

Like Jesus," with his mother accompanying on piano. Gaining confidence at an early age allowed King to think in broad terms about great concepts. Very early in his education, he would speak of great and weighty ideas, and how these would impact on the nation as a whole. Here again, is an example of the grandiloquent style King eventually developed, excerpted from his book, *Where Do We Go From Here: Chaos or Community?*:

"This is the great problem of mankind. We have inherited a large house, a great 'world house' in which we have to live together, black and white, Easterner and Westerner, Gentile and Jew, Catholic and Protestant, Moslem and Hindu, a family unduly separated in ideas, culture and interest, who, because we can never live apart, must live with each other in peace. However deeply American Negroes are caught in the struggle to be at last home in our homeland of the U.S., we cannot ignore the larger world house in which we are also dwellers. Equality with whites will not solve the problems of either whites or Negroes if it means equality in a world society stricken by poverty, and in a universe doomed to extinction by war" (pg. 167).

King's maturity emanated (in a very real way) from his social position within the community headed by his father-who encouraged his son to follow diligently in his footsteps. But his advantage within the church had a downside as well. As the minister's son, King felt special pressures to conform. It is hardly surprising that he began to assert his independence from his father about this time, although he remained respectful of the authority that his father came to represent. This was important to King's personality, because leadership required a certain amount of humility, or at least the appearance of humility. Without authority, there could be no leadership, and leadership was King's highest calling. Therefore, he did not tear away at authority, but came to respect it.

As an eight, one might be surprised to learn that King favored a thoughtful, rather than an emotional approach to religious matters. This might have been a product of his nine wing, which would seek to minimize the conflicts that could result from the rowdy, disorderly interpretations of religious witness exemplified by the revivalists. This is in apparent contradiction with King's eight-nature, though, which could exploit an emotional setting, and would later do so in the civil rights arena. But that is not to say that King sought disorder as an eightpersonality, to attain an advantage in which to lead. On the contrary, he sought to synthesize ideas wherever he could, to preserve order, which is another typical trait of the peacemaker in King.

King's rebellion against established authority and traditional religion was tempered by a desire for reconciliation and a synthesis of conflicting views, a predictable outcome for a nine wing.

In "The Religious Evolution of Martin Luther King, Jr.," Carson points out that King consistently sought to transform rather than abandon the beliefs and practices of the black Baptist religion of his father's generation. King's adoption of liberal religious views set him apart from his father's more orthodox beliefs, and enabled him to think seriously of becoming a minister himself. Determined to assert his independence from his father and questioning aspects of his father's religious beliefs, King, Jr. nevertheless was able to combine the essentials of his theological orientation learned from such teachers as Benjamin Mays and his father's politically engaged ministry and his strong desire to work for social justice.

It is interesting to note that, during his college years, King became increasingly skeptical of the religious liberalism that had been his point of departure from his father's legacy. After all, Carson reminds us in the aforementioned work that King's theological development replicated his childhood: a period during which he resolved conflicting influences by seeking to incorporate the best elements of many alternatives.

King remained on good terms with his father throughout his early adolescence and into his early adulthood. Writing to his father from a summer job in Simsbury, Connecticut, King said, "I am still thinking of the church and reading my bible. And I am not doing any thing that I would not be doing in front of you." Characteristic of King in these years is a searching for truth and synthesis of the emotionalism of his father's biblical interpretation and King's own nine wing, thoughtful contemplation of the more intellectually-satisfying consideration of the harmony between God and his church, and in the environment in general.

King's impressions about his relationships with the white world would be crucial to his work of course; and these were shaped in his early years in the presence of mother and father. In his work, *Stride Toward Freedom*, King recalls an instance when he is riding in the family car and a white policeman pulled up and asked to see his father's license. The cop apparently made a disparaging remark, because King remembers his father replying:

> *"I'm no boy." Pointing to young Martin, the elder King then said, "This is a boy. I'm a man, and until you call me one, I will not listen to you."*

The policeman hurriedly wrote the ticket and disappeared, but would always remain in King's memory as the authority figure who had provoked his father, and who had been brought down a notch by his father's direct, forceful reply. He would describe his father, in his autobiography, as "a real father" who "would always put the family first." He would insist that his father "had never made more than an ordinary salary, but the secret was that he knew the art of saving and budgeting, and never squandered anything, providing the basic necessities of life to the family with little strain" ("The Religious Evolution of King, pg. 17).

Eight With a Nine Wing

As we've mentioned already, King had a nine wing to go with his basic eight personality. His aggressive leadership personality was tempered by the moderate gentleness of the nine, and this might have been due to the influence of his mother, although he was closer to his father.

The traits of the eight and those of a nine wing are in some degree of conflict with each other. Healthy persons of this subtype are noticeably more at ease with themselves and with other people, not feeling that they must assert themselves at every moment or in every situation. Nines are, at times, more open to concerns beyond their immediate self-interest, particularly those involving members of their own family. Eights with a nine wing are the kinder, more benign type, strong willed but mild mannered, who have deeper feelings and more subtle appreciations than eights with a seven-wing, for example. In addition to King, noteworthy examples ofthis subtype—highlighted in Riso's, Personality Types: Using the Enneagram for Self-Discovery—include Golda Meir, Charles de Gaulle, Pablo Picasso, John Huston, Johnny Cash, Fidel Castro, Leonid Brezhnev, Othello and King Lear, to name a few.

One of the clearest signs that King was an eight with a nine wing was his ability to forge a personal (almost mystical) bond between himself and others. During the earliest days of the civil rights campaigns, particularly, King exuded the warmth and strength of character that made people revere him. His speech at the Lincoln Memorial on August 28, 1963, was the high point of his life, and signaled the high-water mark of his ministry. Following this speech, which was aired into the homes of millions of Americans, King achieved a stature that bordered on sainthood. Because it was the era of television, King forged his mystical bond with virtually an entire nation, and they loved him in return. This is the nine wing at work, tempering the aggressive, almost self-centered attributes of the eight, and in return generating respect and even love.

The timing of the speech was historic. The civil rights movement achieved tremendous successes in the rural South, and had now begun to shift its focus on the urban North. The barriers that King and others hoped to tear down were loathsome anyway: lunch counters where only whites could sit, buses in which whites had all the front seats, libraries segregated by race, and worst of all, schools in which poor black children were condemned to a substandard education that would hamper them always in the quest for life's betterment.

To these practices King took aim in his speech, arousing sympathy among a white population who were, generally speaking, deeply offended by the policies of "separate but equal" anyway. King brought a voice which they could understand, and which by this time had achieved a measure of synthesis from the conflicting ideas around him. In true eight style, King brought all of the ideas of all of the various interests together, with him in the lead of course, and articulated the synthesis in an eloquent manner.

The expansive forcefulness of the eight with a nine wing is grounded on some inner fortress of imperturbable strength which others are not allowed to breach. Martin Luther King put that trait to the test during the "mature" phase of the civil rights movement, when many of the first and most objectionable barriers to equality had been already removed.

Many of his followers, both black and white, urged that the time for nonviolence had passed, that the message of liberation in the Sermon on the Mount could not succeed as a "weapon available to oppressed people in their struggle for freedom." Repeatedly King acknowledged that he was finding their arguments increasingly persuasive, their impatience more appealing, and their strategies of direct action more tempting. Yet each time he ended up reaffirming his fundamental commitment to the practicality of his own teachings as a political program for the liberation of American blacks.

King achieved a balance of the eight and the nine wing. Average people of this subtype begin to show a definite split between the two sides of themselves-the aggressive side (which they show in public and in competitive situations) and the passive, more accommodating side. Whether it was the firm upbringing of his early childhood, or whether it was the intellectual nurturing he received during his years at the university, King achieved a rare synthesis of his personality, just as he had achieved synthesis of the emotionalism of his father's approach to religion and his own, more thoughtful approach. Depending on the ninewing's strength, individuals of this subtype are somewhat more oriented to people and less to possessions than the other subtype.

This is very true of King. He clearly identified with anti-elitist values, and remained reluctant throughout his life to associate himself with the values associated with upward economic mobility. King summarizes his view of the socioeconomic ideal by the following statement he makes in his *Autobiography of Religious Development*:

> *"The community in which I was born was characterized with a sort of unsophisticated simplicity. No one in our community was in the extremely poor class. This community was not the slum district. It is probably fair to class the people of this community as those of average income. Yet I insist that this was a wholesome community, notwithstanding the fact that none of us were ever considered members of the "upper class."*

Such attitudes typified his entire ministry. He possessed a high degree of sympathy for poor people and those less fortunate, likely due to his nine wing. King states:

> *"I find myself thinking more and more about what I consider as mankind's second great evil: the evil of poverty. Cannot we agree that the time has indeed come for an all-out war on poverty... in every town and village of the World where this nagging evil exists? We have allowed the poor to become invisible, and we have become angry when they make their presence felt. But just as nonviolence has exposed the ugliness of racial injustice, we must now find ways to expose and heal the sickness of poverty, not just the symptoms, but its basic causes."*

His economic doctrines would eventually get him into trouble with some conservative, possibly reactionary forces within the government. But King did not fear conflict with others. He was comforted by a strong sense of the spiritual, evidenced by the sentiments on pages 134 and 135 of his work,

Stride Toward Freedom, where he reflects on his own "Kitchen Table" experience: "Stand up for righteousness, stand up for truth; and God will be at your side forever."

Eventually, King would call for radical economic reforms, but that was only natural, because of the nine-wing's orientation to people, and not objects. When nine wings are not healthy, they can be ruthless, even destructive. They can become distant and depersonalized. There is no evidence to suggest that King experienced any of these pathologies in his personality.

Although he was a somewhat distant person at times, this was due to his natural sense of inner peace, which he carefully cultivated as a nine wing. Distance is part of this personality type, to some degree. But King never seemed to step over the boundary into aloofness, indifference and bitterness, even when the civil rights movement became more fragmented, and leadership roles changed. King maintained his basic thrust of non-violent action, even when more militant forces counseled less peaceful means to achieve their goals.

His ability to transcend these forces, to maintain his own sense of dignity and self-respect, without disintegrating into either self-destructive or malicious behavior is a great testament to the power of King's Faith in his God, his church and his friends. His greatest gift to us, was of his very self and soul, transformed, redeemed, and shared with all the world.

Conclusion

This poem by a black and unknown bard, quoted throughout his 13-year public ministry by King, summarizes well the rhythms at work in the life-long soul development of this extraordinary human being. And he rendered it magnificently, hundreds of times:

> Fleecy locks and dark complexion,
> Cannot forfeit nature's claim,
> Skin may differ but not affection,

Dwells in black and white the same.

Were I so tall as to reach the pole,

Or to grasp the ocean at a span,

I must be measured by my soul,

The mind is the standard of the man.

Chapter 10

The Beloved Economy: King's True Legacy, and America's Too

A marriage of the ethics of King and the binary economy proposed by Louis Kelso hold the only prospect for a workable society of economic and social justice.

The following lecture was given by the author at Morehouse College in January 1986, as part of its celebration of the first national MLK birthday celebration jointly by the departments of economics and religion, as the Brazeal-Williams Lecture.

There is an important debate and dialogue not taking place within the black church and community. It is about the relationship between religion and economics in the non-violent culture growing out of the legacy of Martin Luther King, Jr.

Part One: Overview

An important aspect of Dr. King's ministry had to do with addressing a nation and a culture about centuries of assault on the life and dignity of an entire race of people, as well as his calculated challenge to the evil triad of racism, war and poverty. An often over-looked aspect of his extraordinary career was his focus on what he stated, on the eve of that fateful night in Memphis, as his conviction that "we as a people would get to the promised land."

He was doing-in what would be his final speech on 3 April 1968-the selfsame thing he had done in his nonviolent inaugural speech at the Holt Street Baptist Church on the night of 5 December 1955. On that last occasion, the statement, "we as a people" was his concluding word and testament to the entire world.

During those years of action-oriented ministry, King had to take on an entire nation, with less time than he really needed to address the internal and developmental needs of the black community itself. Seven years before his death, he stated that sense of neglect as a chief source of frustration for himself and the movement.

Thus, we are just now getting down in a serious way to that long neglected dialogue on the relationship between religion and economics in the non-violent revolution.

There has been another fairly vigorous debate taking place in some comers of the black church. It concerns the relevancy of black theology, black religion, and the struggle of black Americans for justice. This second, less urgent but no less important debate continues to take place within the more limited ranks of black theologians and scholars, and one dare not overlook the lessons of that literature (Gayrud S. Wilmore and James H. Cone, *Black Theology: A Documentary History, 1966-1979*, New York: Orbis).

I believe that there are critical perspectives missing from the black Theology debate (as useful as it has been) which renders it less useful for practitioners of a serious ministry of economic and spiritual transformation of black America.

Let me characterize that absent quality as the willingness, or rather "unwillingness" to "do theology" in such a way as it could help in the black church's historical mission: to feed hungry stomachs and to feed hungry hearts. That is certainly a reasonable expectation, given the mandate of Him who calls us to give the hungry "loaves of bread and not stones of talk"

My perspective is that of a long-time participant/observer in the civil rights movement, and as a serious student and disciple of Martin Luther King, Jr., who served on his national board before and during the rise of the black power, black theology debate. It was also that of a local community activist and pastor in an innovative, inner-city demonstration parish in a major northern city during the sixties, where I learned very soon that there could be no separation of "feeding hungry stomachs" from "feeding hungry hearts." Hungry people need a demonstration of love and lifting, before they can even hear a sermon on "love lifting me."

The dire economic plight of the masses of our people, as I witnessed it in that city, had caught my deep interest as I toiled at what we styled ... an economic and spiritual ministry. This was the stated mission and goal of The Blue Hill Christian Center and Parish in the Roxbury section of Boston from 1963 to 1971. A large part of my time and effort during those same years was in putting together the development group for the Boston OIC, and serving several years as Dr. Leon Sullivan's Southern Regional Director; assisting in founding and establishing 13 OIC's in eight states. Then too, SCLC was in preparation for its Poor People's Campaign, and the opportunity Dr. King gave me in 1968 to address a forum of 1,200 black preachers from across the land afforded me the chance to share some of my different ideas about how black Americans might wage a fight for economic parity. Moreover, the Lord used me in facilitating a meeting between Dr. King and Mr. Louis O. Kelso, whom I believed at that time had developed a major plan—which could be a practical model for bringing about an economic transformation in black America, similar to the result produced in the post-Pentecost community described in the Acts of the Apostles (Acts 4:32).

Augmenting that seminal interest with intense study, both formal and informal, I pursued some studies in economics, and in the emerging science of organization development while obtaining my doctorate at the Harvard University Graduate School of Education (1970-73). That furlough enabled me to do some in-depth reflection on how I believed God had been using Martin Luther King and his ministry. An additional opportunity to serve as dean and director of a major white university's minority student support effort left me with the deep down conviction that white America—in its second generation of post-King activity-had much of black America's intellectual leadership (and our leadership in preparation) trapped in a revolving door of busyness, very active but going nowhere soon.

Through all these years, and with further reflection, research, and much dialogue with black theologians, black economists, and many black pastors, I have arrived at the conclusion that there is but one road left to black Americans by which we can have any real hope of going beyond survival to development.

That road entails for us, as a people, a deliberate decision for self-development, augmented by whatever help is ever available to us from outside sources. Whoever is in the White House at any given time, or whatever the general disposition to black advancement might be, our constant must be that deliberate decision for self-development by the full mobilization, utilization, and leveraging of every resource, human and non-human, available to us as a people for economic and spiritual transformation.

In The Origins of the Civil Rights Movement, Aldon Morris presented the first major study of that movement employing "an indigenous perspective" as part of its methodology. Morris comes to a similar conclusion in his section on the impact of the Civil Rights movement.

A critical question confronting the black community today is whether the organizations, leadership, tactics, and philosophies of the civil rights movement are appropriate for bringing about basic economic change, or whether a whole new set of structures and tactics is needed. The civil rights movement suggests some basic lessons regarding prospects for change. (Aldon Morris, *The Origins of the Civil Movement*, New York, The Free Press, 1984, p. 29)

Of the three lessons he proposes, I am mainly in agreement with the middle one, that "if a successful struggle for economic justice is to occur, it will require a high level of internal organization that uses all of the resources of the black community."

The debate that should have taken place back in 1967 during the preparation for the Poor People's Campaign and the rising consciousness about where we were then (essentially between the black Theology Movement and the Martin Luther King Non-Violent Revolution) is-as James Cone says-about the search for "an authentic word from the Christian God for black Americans and other oppressed people." And I say, if that word for the disinherited and oppressed comes through Martin Luther King's legacy, and through the Jesus tradition of the Old and New Testaments, then that word will be the Theology of jubilee: a theology beyond all particularities, ethnic and otherwise ... a way for the poor to move from oppression and disinheritance to justice and ownership, indeed a marriage of ethics and economics.

Part Two: A Black Community Moves Toward a Beloved Community

The Montgomery movement almost 50 years ago represented the beginning of black people as a "community-of-the-whole," exercising a number of new, very critical linkages.

Just at the outset of King's work in Montgomery in 1955, every level of black life in America was absolutely quiescent before the dehumanizing system, which segregated and brutalized us all, regardless of our socio-economic situation or status.

Today, there has been the shaking of the foundation of that system by every stratum within the black community-in distinct, reverberating waves. Such waves have involved the black wealthy, whose independence should be greatest given their larger number of life chances and options, all the way to the black jail class, whose life chances are about nil. The latter have been subjected to the most aggravated repression, with no economic breathing space. One can measure the healthiness or sickness of public policy in terms of its direct impact on the size of these groups. For example, public policy determines that the black working class is growing smaller with fewer jobs available, while the jail class is becoming larger.

Now, after 44 years of apprenticeship in the modem-day civil rights movement, we still find ourselves trapped in isolation from each other. Witness the degree of hostility often present between the masses and the other black classes, which historically was overcome in Montgomery when middle class doctors' wives became drivers for working class maids to their jobs. The greatest hope for the black-community-of-the-whole is to find its opportunity and responsibility in the linkages, which give it handles for transforming its needs into an aggregated market for its own purposes of moving towards economic independence, and interdependence.

This is the clearest point at which the black-community-of-the-whole can seek to transform its liabilities, or inequities and needs, into a massive new set of assets. That a clear majority of our black masses are in prison or trapped in the 'jail of welfare" constitutes a situation that black people cannot afford and America is not likely to tolerate for too much longer.

Such conditions constitute a time bomb, ticking away at the base of black survival in America. It is no less than the choice between the life and death of a people. Either the full development of black people as a viable sector within the American economic setting will take place, or the continual destruction and unmaking of us as a people is a certainty. However, when one does a critical analysis of the balance sheet, setting black assets against black liabilities, it becomes crystal clear that black people could create a new future for themselves, a "turnabout" to economic health and viability.

Part Three: The Dream Team Within

As in Montgomery, a black church, town, and gown Dream Team partnership is a necessary condition for establishing a Beloved Community in our present day situation. In Montgomery, the role of the black church has been clearly documented. What is less well understood is the role of black professors, university administrators, and students in that setting, as well as the response of black professionals, labor leaders, and business persons. Indeed, it seems that when they all stood up together, the whole black community was on the move, as with one common mind, one purpose, one spirit (i.e., common market, mind, and money-commonwealth).

I have borrowed the name Dream Team from that of Virginia Union University's winning basketball team of the 1940's and 50's.

In the Dream Team of the Beloved Community, the black church becomes the spiritual tie, black educators represent the potential community brain trust, and the black community-of-the-whole is the setting and the matrix within which either confusion will continue to reign, or within which this new partnership, when effected, would doggedly work towards its economic and social recovery. The black American situation is an economic case with its own history, context, contradictions, and peculiar challenges. It is likely that only when there is a significant movement growing from within the agony of the black economic crisis for non-violent resolution, will there be found any real and workable solutions.

At this point, the organizational development potential among black nationwide organizations functioning at local levels fails to coalesce significantly for resolving the critical problems facing the masses of black people. These organizations crisscross the country year after year, missing the opportunity to synergize their efforts toward the economic and social betterment of their people. At the national meetings, some very fine initiatives get hammered out and resolutions and programs set, which may or may not get back to the local level. Suppose a half dozen or more of these organizations married themselves to one another back at the local level and brought all of their national organizations' initiatives to the table for joint work on implementation, It could be a new day very soon.

Another reason these organizations now fail to synergize their efforts is that the organizational framework around which they function engenders high levels of competitiveness and inter-group rivalry. What is required for the economic survival and development of black people and our communities is that a new set of cooperative relationships be made at the local community level. These new relationships would center around helping lift the masses, and helping those organizations and their broad professional memberships find new and useful outlets.

A greater entrepreneurial approach to solving these problems would also result in vastly increased job opportunities for the black professional and manager, as well as the ordinary worker. When the appropriate organizational development framework is achieved, it will afford all a total win situation, and will bring together the black classes and the black masses in a brand new appreciation for each other.

We must gather new black resources even as we challenge the nation to become partners with the black-community-of-the-whole in this great adventure. When we assess our needs and our resources, the conclusion is inescapable. The resources, actual and potential, could begin to match the needs and liabilities. It is no longer the question of whether we can in fact develop their economic sector. What is required is the will to begin, a plan, and the commitment and guts to see it through to takeoff and beyond.

Moreover, it is time to recognize that if the nation desires to put racism effectively behind itself, and to participate in the dream, then it will have to follow where King, led so sacrificially, to eradicate the residual results and inequities of racism, both institutional and individual.

In every local community that desires to lift itself to the status of a Beloved Community with a strong economic and a vibrant spiritual base, there must emerge this Dream Team partnership, and it will usually be convened by the black church. However, the initiative could come from the gown or the town.

Through such an effort, the black-community-of-the-whole invites and welcomes a broad participation by persons from all over America, as part of a spiritual awakening to new opportunities to show how great our na-tion and its people could be. It is to say with assurance, that we as a total people can so focus our minds and souls on a set of opportunities and crises, that in this place we can create the America that persons in every place desire for themselves. And all the rest of us—who are blessed not to be hungry, or in jail, or physically, emotionally or mentally broken—will direct our energies of mind, money and markets so that people and communities not so well blessed can stand firmly on their own two feet.

Part Four: the Black Church as the Economic Development Catalyst

The black church has long been painfully aware of the reality concerning black economic well-being. A relatively small handful of black people have made modest gains while the vast majority of the black masses are worse off, in relative and absolute terms, than at any time during the seventies and eighties.

The black church during the past several years has stepped up its efforts to find a way of assisting various groups in articulating their economic aspirations in such a way that all can legitimately prosper, while helping most to lift those farthest down. It is the task, strenuous but rewarding, of lifting one's brothers and sisters as one also climbs. At its most refined level, it is the art of inducing and encouraging all to lift and climb together.

Many are the researchers on the subject of black poverty. Historically, they have assaulted this problem in isolation from each other. Recently, these individuals have found themselves broadening their circle of discussion, the dialogue becoming more inter-disciplinary, and the debate more focused. Fortunately, it is now moving to the local community level.

The legitimate needs of our community together constitute a kind of "death valley situation," especially for the masses of our people: youth, the elderly, single parent families and prisoners. Many groups are beginning to focus their minds on how the black church, in cooperation with other black institutions, can effectively serve as a dynamic and catalytic agent in the economic development of black America, and it must!

Black people, whenever we decide to stop doing what one spiritual statesman has called "jitter-bugging on Martin's grave," we will follow the spirit and truth of Dr King, and do all we can, while at the same time, call on America to do what it must to fulfill the dream!

This is not to say that black people will seek to develop communities as exclusive property for themselves. It is to say that we black people will take major responsibility for our own self-development, including reducing the need for welfare as a major support system for the masses of people, and the development of a network of institutions for the spiritual restoration of our people and their communities. Growing out of this effort would be: a) the eventual un-jailing of prisoners, making them productive as an alternative to their present lives; b) turning off our youth from the crippling and debilitating use of drugs, and onto their own selfactualizing potential; c) overcoming community crime. All these goals constitute a major challenge to a Beloved Community economic development effort.

At the same time that black people go from self-help to selfdevelopment through a Beloved Community economic development movement, governments of national, state and city administrations will need to channel a portion of the resources presently being spent very badly for the needs outlined here. If the nation is really serious about reducing the social problems about which its leaders rail, then it now has the challenge of black people's willingness to take the responsibility for the turnabout of black America.

The black church must be the catalyst. King tapped into the true self-understanding which the black church has of itself and which Peter Paris describes in his book, *The Social Teaching of the Black Churches*, as "an embodiment of communal power." What black America has variously called "soul force," "moral suasion," "moderation," and "non-violence," Paris chooses to call "communal power" because of an implicit drive for unity between contending parties. "Communal power is a force that recognizes the potentiality for community and strives unceasingly for its realization. It is the essence of communal power to sustain the potentiality for communal relationships, regardless of the circumstances" (Peter J. Paris, *The Social Teaching of the Black Churches*, Philadelphia: Fortress Press, 1985, pgs. 115-127).

As already indicated, due to the oppressive and repressive nature of American Jim Crow racism of the post World War II years, Dr. King had to spend a disproportionate amount of time and emphasis overcoming these conditions. He was unable to address the problems and prospects regarding the internal development of black America adequately, nor to focus the massive machinery of the civil rights movement on such internal development.

However, at this point, we have no choice but to mobilize the full economic and spiritual potential embodied in the communal power of the black church for the survival and development of our people and their communities. When the black church does focus the same kind of leadership, resources, and planning for the economic and spiritual transformation of our people and communities as it did in fighting Jim Crow, we will in all probability experience a dramatic improvement in our plight within a short span of time. Dr. King was a man for his people, a man for his country, and a man for his world.

Here I have concentrated on his work of creating the Beloved Community in that arena where the black church has the direct exercise of power and influence. It does not need to convince any power outside itself before taking on the critical situation and the crying needs of black people, which can only be resolved by a major movement aimed at the internal self-development of its people and their communities.

We could think of this as one aspect of the dream—its challenge and developmental possibilities among his own people, without denying the wider implications of his work or his dream, for either his country or his world.

PART FIVE: The Economic and Spiritual Foundations of the Beloved Community

The life, words, and work of King as the continuing dream, when lived and lifted by the many thousands of those who show themselves committed, can bring about the economic and spiritual transformation of our communities into the Beloved Community.

The King dream, when internalized by those who now cherish his legacy, becomes an overpowering vision making for the actual experience of living in the Beloved Community. The Beloved Community, in its idealized version, is a thing of beauty; but when it becomes the daily agenda of persons, organizations and institutions within unlovely, decaying communities for whom he lived and died, it will take on new life and vitality, economic soundness and viability, with new spirit and visibility.

The power yet contained in the dream, when focused and directed by the Dream Team, can bring about real life benefits, participation, and joy as a Beloved Community-in-waiting.

When an ordinary community does in fact become a Beloved Community, the influence and leadership of the Dream Team will be felt in those streets where Dr. King surely would have given lift to the homeless and hungry. In those streets from which his blood yet cries, we still have a choice and a chance. The choice is whether to vindicate his suffering by healing that of millions still suffering needlessly; the chance is to bring the Beloved Community to every community.

When a community becomes a Beloved Community, then all its people-the haves and the have-nots, serving each other and being served by each other-will affirm it, celebrate it, and work to sustain and maintain its on-going life for self, others, nature and God.

In his book, *Jesus Through the Centuries*, Jaroslav Pelikan gives his analysis of King's concept of the Beloved Community. Based on that assessment of Dr. King's place in the history of culture, he moves the argument away from the integration and love themes, which characterize most critiques of the King mind, such as Ansbro's, and toward justice as the end-point for our struggle with power. I offer the following rather extensive quote:

> *"In his own series of nonviolent campaigns over the next decade, Martin Luther King put that philosophy to the test. Even many of his followers, both black and white, urged that the time for nonviolence had passed, that the message of liberation in the Sermon on the Mount could not succeed as a 'weapon available to oppressed people in their struggle for freedom.'*
>
> *Repeatedly, he acknowledged that he was finding their arguments increasingly*

persuasive, their impatience more appealing, their strategies of direct action more tempting. Yet each time he ended up reaffirming his fundamental commitment to the practicality of the teachings of the Sermon on the Mount as a political program for the liberation of American blacks. At the heart of this program was the vision of human society as a Beloved Community. He described this community at length especially in his book Stride Toward Freedom.

It was to be a society in which-within the standard triad of justice, power, and love-the historic definition of justice would gradually become a reality through the moderation of power by love. He knew it would not happen all of sudden, and he was realistic enough to recognize that there would be many individuals whom the evangelical imperatives of love would not change; only law, and the enforcement of law, could do that. But he had learned from Gandhi that "mere interaction between individuals' was not, despite centuries of Christian interpretation, the deepest meaning of 'the love ethic of Jesus."

Rather, the love ethic would have to penetrate and reform the structure of society itself and, through those structures, create a context of love and justice to which, through power, even the recalcitrant would have to conform" (Jaroslav Pelikan, Jesus Through the Centuries, His Place in the History of Culture, New Haven: Yale University Press, 1985, pg. 217).

I cannot remember ever hearing Dr. King making such a reference to the biblical jubilee or actually using the term jubilee in any of his speeches or conversations. In a conversation with Mrs. King, the author learned that she also cannot remember his ever having used the term in reference to his own work.

When I was 18 years old-at the end of my first year as a student at Virginia Union University-during the summer, my home church gave me the assignment of getting notes on its history from the one man in the community whose memory went back the farthest among all the elders of the community. He was just about at his 94th birthday. He had been about ten or eleven years old, according to his story, at the time when Lincoln signed the

Emancipation Proclamation. He stated that all the slaves rejoiced greatly at receiving the news of the emancipation, and usually spoke of it at length as the great jubilee taking place, with jubilee as the central meaning and metaphor explaining what had happened. And they talked of it repeatedly.

Through a lifetime of growing up—despite studying in college, seminary and graduate school—the author rarely heard the term used except that occasionally it would appear as a passing reference in a few limited technical theology books, but almost never in the common parlance of the church setting.

More recently, the literature has begun to build around the subject and—in my own estimation—this started with the scholarly work of the late Johannes Hoekendijk, former professor of Missiology at Union Seminary in New York. Worth reading is his inaugural address on the jubilee as, "missions the celebration of freedom," and published in the Union Seminary Quarterly Review in 1966. More recently, with the republishing of Andre Trocme's book, *Jesus and the Nonviolent Revolution*, it has become even clearer that the biblical concept of jubilee embodies the teachings of Jesus on non-violence and combines the ethical and economic requirements for a just society. It provides mechanisms for the establishment of justice over time, and the reversal of injustice, which most assuredly builds up over time. As such, this book must become part of our literature for concentrated study, along with the books written by Dr. King, for we must seek to remember not only what he said and did, but also the message buried within his language.

It is important for us to determine whether the jubilee was a part of the cultural memory for the contemporary black church and Martin Luther King: that even without the term being used, its biblical formulation was powerfully at work during the civil rights movement.

Robert N. Bellah and others, writing in *Habits of the Heart*, report on their conversations with a wide range of diverse Americans. The fundamental question that they posed and which was repeatedly posed to them was "how to preserve or create a morally coherent life" (Robert N. Bellah,

Richard Madsen, William Sullivan, Ann Swidler, and Steven Tipton, *Habits of the Heart*, Los Angeles: University of California Press, 1985). In their effort to trace and understand the role of individualism and commitment in American life, they share a very savvy conclusion both about the nature of cultural memory, and about the strategic and critical impact of Martin Luther King's words and work:

> *"To remind us of what is possible, we may call to mind one of the most significant social movements of recent times, a movement overwhelmingly religious in its leadership that changed the nature of American society. Under the leadership of Martin Luther King, Jr., the civil rights movement called upon Americans to transform their social and economic institutions with the goal of building a just national community that would respect both the differences and the interdependence of its members. It did this by combining biblical and republican themes in a way that included, but transformed, the culture of individualism.*

Juxtaposing the poetry of the scriptural prophets ... with the lyrics of patriotic anthems ... King's oration re-appropriated that classic stand of the American tradition that understands the true meaning of freedom to lie in the affirmation of responsibility for uniting all of the diverse members of society into a just social order. For King, the struggle for freedom became a practice of commitment within a vision of America as a community of memory."

Yes, Dr. King drew on the American community of memory for his dream for all America and the black church community of memory for his ethic of jubilee.

PART SIX: Building a Comprehensive Belvoed Community... and Another and Another

To Do the Work is to Accept the Greatest Challenge of All

We must do it because he brought us far enough to see that the good society can be made to work. The vision was his, as was the undying confidence in its ultimate achievement. In the spring of 1965, Dr. King said it best himself:

> *"I find myself thinking more and more about what I consider as mankind's second great evil: the evil of poverty. Cannot we agree that the time has indeed come for an all-out war on poverty ...in every town and village of the world where this nagging evil exists? We have allowed the poor to become invisible, and we have become angry when they make their presence felt. But just as nonviolence has exposed the ugliness of racial injustice, we must now find ways to expose and heal the sickness of poverty, not just the symptoms, but its basic causes."*

Thus, an appropriate church-and-community-based development consortium, serving as an economic development catalyst in convening all the appropriate community and power sectors of any willing urban community, could facilitate the development of a living community, which would be built around the ethics of King and incorporate compatible economic designs such as those of Louis O. Kelso.

Mr. Louis O. Kelso, the former San Francisco corporate and financial lawyer and economist—author (with Patricia Retter Kelso) of *Two Factor Theory: The Economics of Reality* (1967), and *Democracy and Economic Power: Extending the ESOP Revolution* (1986), and several other books on the subject of alternatives for capital growth and expanding capital ownership among those without ownership of productive capital in our society—laid the groundwork for such significant development.

These new community developments would be a living answer to the challenge expressed above by Dr. King himself, and posed in the title of his book, *Where do we go from Here: Chaos or Community?* For many persons of the local church and the surrounding area, such new communities would be seen as drawing heavily on the ethical principles of Jesus Christ as articulated and exemplified by King.

Kwanza Jubilee as a Cultural Construct for "The New Community"

Kwanza Jubilee is the most appropriate metaphor for the new community, and as such, it is designed to link two very powerful streams in the experience of black Americans. Kwanza means "first fruits." It is the celebration of the first harvest of the crops, when harvesters come together to make joyful festivities, to give thanks and to enjoy the blessings of living and acting together for the benefit of the larger community. Everyone brings what he or she grew or made to the Karamu Feast of the Celebration. Jubilee is a biblical expression of the vision of peace, justice and equity. It is also the term chosen by liberated, Christian black slaves, after the Emancipation Proclamation of 1865, to express how they felt about their new status, as was noted earlier.

Kwanza Jubilee combines these two powerful traditions to signal a profound meaning to a wide range of persons in the black community (and in many other communities) as well as to provide the important link of the generations, with the older people more oriented to the notion of jubilee, and the younger, to Kwanza. As a concept, it also summons all who believe, as did Dr. King, that the dream was only the first step in creating a new society.

Role of the Churches

For years, the local black church has realized its vital role in the development of the community that it serves. The church is outstanding in this tradition. The black church recognizes that its efforts of the past, however effective, have too often been those of single parishes (often "Lone Ranger" types), and hence their effectiveness has not produced the results that the present critical situation requires. In considering the economic development of cities and rural areas together, it is important to consider the church in the aggregate sense, as developed by Dr. King. For example, during the sixties, "Operation Breadbasket" was mainly a coordinated program of the churches to use their combined muscle to secure employment and fuller economic participation for black people and their institutions within the framework of major corporate America.

A further dimension to the breadbasket-type approach would be the use of local, church-convened, Beloved Community foundations to create the thrust towards effective community development, such as land aggregation, sponsorship of new enterprise development and the local organization of people for personal, family and community growth.

This is envisioned as a dual program consisting of a major physical development in the community, coupled with the human restoration of persons in the process. Moreover, Beloved Community foundations are aimed at creating viable and self-sustaining inner city economies, making possible the further development of the potentialities of people and community. Their initial aim would be to catalyze a movement of social development that could overcome the pathologies of unemployment, drugs, crime, alienation, apathy and the like.

This would be accomplished through a network of churches and community organizations providing links to existing services in the areas of day care, health, manpower and jobs, community prison reform and rehabilitation, family strengthening, housing management, consumer education and practices, adult education, youth development, work for and with the elderly, etc. Social development would take place through the specialization in each social problem by a group of churches and organizations taken from the total group within the aggregate body of the Beloved Community foundation.

For example, four of the total number of churches might choose the work of youth hooked on drugs, having their elderly members involved in helping turn these youths off drugs and dope, and onto their own self-actualizing potential. Naturally, the major side benefit of making the community a desirable and wholesome place to live is the fact that it also makes it a more desirable and attractive place to invest, and makes it affordable for present residents, as well.

The Partnership involved

The major organizations involved in developing the New community would be: (1) 12-15+ church-based incorporating sponsors; (2) a community-based joint-venture planning and economic development group; (3) a major real estate development company with proven effectiveness and compatible philosophy; and (4) existing business organizations and institutions in the area. An organizational development approach should be undertaken in which all the power sectors sit at the table of challenge and opportunity, each to give and receive as is appropriate and consonant with the ethics of King.

The churches, representing the spiritual and organizing sector, must be coequally joined with the banks and insurance companies and other investors, the chamber of commerce and private enterprise, government at all levels, the residents through their community foundation, and other outside groups desiring to be part of this great adventure to create a "community within a community" as an economic and moral alternative to the conditions which now exist.

The Physical Plan

The Beloved Community foundation development would be planned to include residential, industrial, and commercial projects, integrated around a total plan for the economic turnabout of the area.

The Financial Plan

The creation of these communities is to be achieved in such a way that incentives are built into the very process of their development for all those involved. It will be a total win situation for every level of participation. For the present and future residents, beyond reviving their own neighborhoods, will share in new jobs, stabilize old jobs, increase ownership of homes and businesses, and share in the larger equity pie through a rational, fail-safe plan, which all sectors find workable and harmonious. The components to a proposed financial plan are envisioned as follows:

1. The Economic Model– the Kelso Two-Factor Model brings to community development new approaches that are uniquely innovative in both concept and design (i.e., the design of organizational structures, legal relationships, ownership rights, and financing devices that stimulate federal, state, and other public and private investment in housing and economic development). This approach channels investment in a manner that will provide community residents with meaningful job and capital ownership stakes in the profit-making aspects of construction, community economic development, and urban renewal). Many U.S. congressional leaders have embraced the Kelso System and because of this, it has become a key ingredient in several pieces of major legislation.

More than 10,000 U.S. corporations have sold to their employees billions in shares, and financed them according to Kelsonian mechanisms. Kelso had, before his death in 1991, also designed some preliminary models for new community development financing according to these mechanisms.

2. An Early Track Record– the Beloved Community foundation will need to create or establish its credibility early on as it builds towards its own viability. Thus, the need is recognized for an early and visible suc-

cess to help make believers of skeptics and of those who will contribute to later rounds of larger successes. To do this, the foundation should seek to purchase, with Kelsonian mechanisms, several existing firms with annual revenues in excess of several million dollars, either within the locale or beyond it. Such companies should include, over the course of time: a building material company; a food store chain; a medical supply house; fast food chains; landscape nurseries; a trucking company, etc.

3. Planned and Unplanned Alternatives– to say that the foundation would utilize a new approach is a more general way of saying that with a range of alternatives in focus, its ultimate plan will be fashioned in the "rough and tumble" of creating the foundation. The flexibility of our approach would result, I believe, in the choice of some of the alternatives already set forth, and in other cases, variations on the general theme.

4. The Nature of Investment– While it will be the commitment of private investment dollars that will make the Beloved Community foundation project "go," it will be the commitment of "soft" dollars for overhead operations which will be required to supplement the hard investment dollars. This will ultimately assure the long-range success of the program.

However, it must be understood—even at this early stage—that every public dollar, every foundation, church or government cent, must be treated as an investment in the development of human and community restoration. This will eventually provide a return back to the public coffers in the form of higher income taxes paid by workers and capital gains taxes paid by stockholders, as well as lower costs for "social and conflict management" by the government.

For example, whereas it now costs the government about $30,000+ per year to keep a person incarcerated in prison, once that person acquires a skill and a new level of economic participation in a Beloved Community foundation, no longer would that cost (or those for keeping his family on welfare) be required. From a tax-taker, he/she becomes a taxpayer. Once this becomes standard practice in our cities and rural areas, the governmental costs of such "institutional keeping" will fall dramatically, and those monies will be invested elsewhere.

An International Link

The New community interface with other areas and regions is considered a vital part of the concept and, therefore, it must be programmed as such from the start. The significance here derives in part from the important relationship that can exist between U.S. cities and the urban and rural areas of Africa.

While the analogy between urban and rural America and its African counterparts requires careful study, it is introduced here as a pertinent and fundamental element of the new development process.

Why Must This Be Done, And Why Now?

The questions of why and why now ultimately is a story about successful results. A good plan is one that is realistic and highly predictive of success. This plan would be designed with special attention to the question of predictable consequences. It will consider such questions as: how do we strengthen the probabilities for positive consequences at every step in the total process? What are the contingency programs for dealing with the unintended negative consequences when they occur?

Thus, a special impact evaluation instrument would be developed to measure three areas: the economic and financial, the social and community, and the environmental. The general impact evaluation would assess the project's replicability, cost-benefit, cost-efficiency and value engineering analysis. All these will be measured within the range of economic viability and ethical vitality. More specifically, the project's replicability will be a function of at least the following factors:

1. A refocusing of public resources that would envision the expenditures not necessarily of massively larger public dollars, but rather, the strategic use of those already being spent;

2. One major corporation per community, of Fortune-500 size, by creating as part of its own business expansion a development company, with Kelso two-factor economic mechanisms to leverage private capital and other corporate resources;

3. The inclusion of appropriate communications systems and cultural programs, consonant with the overall development theme predicated on King ethics and Kelso economics; and

4. A Beloved Community foundation team willing to share its experience at organizing and implementing the project with teamsin-formation in other cities.

Part Seven: Conclusion

Each of us must eventually attempt what the late Bishop Pike called "doing theology" in the context of a local geography, on one's home turf.

The challenge for us is to rethink our assumptions and basic strategies for change, and to go from reactive confrontation to proactive social and economic problem solving.

Can there be a legitimate marriage between religion and economics? If so, then when and how is the courtship to begin?

For me, this answer is best framed by Jesus the Christ, who fed multitudes of people with almost nothing to work with. King with his ethics of jubilee, and economist Louis Kelso with his "economics of abundance" (versus scarcity) made the same contribution.

Moreover, we have talked about a theology of inclusion-a theology beyond all ethnic particularities.

However, to talk endlessly about the Beloved Community is useless. Even if we should speak about it with the tongues of "men and of angels," but fail to work our love, we have "become sounding brass and a tinkling cymbal" (I Corinthians 13: 1).

King with his life, words and work, conceptualized the Beloved Community with brilliance, proclaimed it with power, and laid its foundations with love.

Now, we can build on it. Because of his uncommon commitment, we must build it. Because of the due diligence of our fore bearers, we must build it. Because our children and our children's children may be naked, hungry, windblown and homeless without it, we must build it. Because without it, none of us could know the purpose and the joy we will surely have with it.

We must erect the Beloved Community with diligence and unwavering commitment. Robert Winfrey, another Morehouse alumnus, says it musically and poetically in his nationally acclaimed song, "Let's Build a City" (or, nation)

144

Let's build a city where all people can live-
free, safe, and in peace.
Let's build a city where ev'ry child can
grow and become as great as he can be.

We can make this land a place of dignity
Sharing our resources for humanity—Come!
Let's build a city-a city of worth
and we'll give birth to a kingdom on earth.
Let's build a city where there is brotherhood
In ev'ry race and creed.
Let's build a city where in each neighborhood
There are friends helping those who're in need.
No more hungry people, no more poverty—
Open ev'ry heart. Let us brothers be.
Come! Let's build a city — a city of worth
And we'll give birth to a kingdom on earth.
Caring for each other, loving one another.

Always standing by to lift a fallen brother-sister
Come! Let's build a city — a city of worth
And we'll give birth to a kingdom on earth.

*Words and music by Robert Wirifrey (Morehouse '54) music department, Boston
Public Schools, founder and former director, Roland Hayes School of Music.*

Chapter 11

Footprints of Mother Rosa

Mrs. Parks, leading a nation in search of its soul.

Rosa Parks has been called the "mother of the civil rights movement" because it was she who refused to move to the back of a city bus in Montgomery, Alabama on December 1, 1955. In the cover leaf of Quiet Strength, Gregory J. Reed reminds us all that with her simple act of courage," ... she set in motion a chain of events that changed forever the landscape of American race relations."

From what has been written about Rosa Parks, one feature of her character shows through most clearly. She is a woman at peace with herself and her world. She is unified in that peace in courage. She has integrated it thoroughly into her character, and indeed, it is her character.

She is a person is best described with the word serene. Her serenity sustained her through trying times from her earliest childhood in Montgomery, the capital of Alabama where Rosa lived, to her pivotal role in the civil rights movement, beginning with her refusal to give up her seat on a Montgomery bus in December 1955. This act launched the Montgomery Bus Boycott, and secured her place and history and her future as a civil rights activist.

Rosa Parks has many qualities: She has nurtured her intellect. She has shown an activist's ambition to dominate events, she has shown a firm resolve as a reformer, at times; and she has shown leadership qualities. Her dominant quality, however, is her placid nature, and the serenity of her mind. This is revealed in her Quiet Strength collection of sayings and favorite quotes (1994). From this simple volume, one obtains a clear picture of a mind brimming with thoughtful observations on her world, and a mind that is focused on maintaining a peaceful outlook.

As a child, she learned to turn to the Bible book of Psalms to hold her peace when she is troubled. Her favorite is Psalm 27 (verses 1-7):

> *"The Lord is my light and my salvation; whom shall I fear? The Lord is the strength of my life; of whom shall I be afraid? When the wicked, even mine enemies and my foes came upon me, to eat up my flesh, they stumbled and fell.*
>
> *Though a host may encamp against me, my heart shall not fear; Though war should rise against me, in this will I be confident..."*

It is within her character to seek this inner peace, and to be sustained by it, so that she may sustain others by it. This leads us to another aspect of her character, namely her idealistic streak, which makes her want to improve the world in whatever way she can. This is a passion; however, the passion is under control: It is focused. The placid nature of her character is what focuses the fiery reformer nature of her character. Rosa Parks exhibits these characteristics.

Based on observations from books by and about Rosa Parks, we can make the case, that in the Enneagram system, Rosa Parks is a nine with a one wing.

The Enneagram

The Enneagram is a methodology for understanding personality types. The Enneagram is like a map: It helps to discover a workable personality typology (a way of classifying human nature) which is accurate and practical. The Enneagram has a long history, dating back to 2500 BC in Babylon or elsewhere in the Middle East. There are nine major personality types in the Enneagram, as shown in figure 1.

The Enneagram model is ancient; SoulScope® has developed a particular application for the application to Soul knowledge and building the beloved community. You can access this wisdom also at SoulScope.com and would profit by knowing your own profile through the on-line profiler.

Let's begin by seeing that the Enneagram describes nine distinct personalities, with unique motivations, strengths and weaknesses. Soul Scope describes these fully in our website SoulScope.com and you will find more detailed information than will now be given in this chapter. The first level is to understand the three triads which make up different motivation and energy sources of the types.

The Enneagram is an entire system of personality analysis. For more,

THE TRIADS

THE ENNEAGRAM

FIGURE ONE

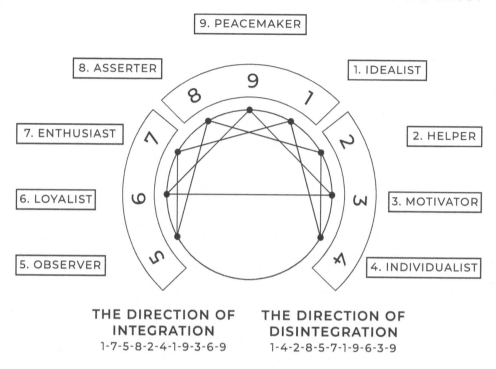

THE DIRECTION OF
INTEGRATION
1-7-5-8-2-4-1-9-3-6-9

THE DIRECTION OF
DISINTEGRATION
1-4-2-8-5-7-1-9-6-3-9

FIGURE TWO

refer to Personality Types: Using the Enneagram for Self-Discovery, Don Richard Riso. The general idea of the Enneagram is that there are nine basic personality "types," and each one of us fits one major type more than any other. The nine types are categorized as numbers. Thus, the one is the reformer, the two is the helper, the three is the status seeker, etc. The following brief descriptions of each type are helpful and demonstrate the highly evolved characteristics as well as the lower, trapped functions of the same type:

The one is principled, orderly, perfectionistic, and rigid.
The two is caring and generous but can be possessive and
manipulative.

The three is self-assured, competitive, type-A, obsessed with
    image and deceitful.

The four is creative, intuitive, introverted, and depressive

The five is wise, perceptive, analytic, emotionally remote,
    detached from people.

The six is likable, dutiful, plagued by doubt, fearful.

The seven is imaginative, an epicure, impulsive, distracted,
    hedonistic.

The eight is self-confident, forceful, combative; can be destructive.

The nine is peaceful, reassuring, passive, may be neglectful at times,
    stubbornly removed.

These are the general traits of each personality type, although the complete description quickly becomes very detailed. In addition to the basic typology, each personality is constantly moving in his or her "direction of integration" or "direction of disintegration." The solid lines on the Enneagram represent directions of integration and disintegration. "Healthy" individuals are always moving in their direction of integration while unhealthy people are disintegrating. For example, the one's direction of integration is to seven, where he or she takes on certain characteristics of the seven, while the one's direction of disintegration is to four, where he or she takes on the unhealthy traits of this personality type.

Rosa Parks in the Enneagram System: The Peacemaker

[This section relies heavily on Don Richard Riso's *Personality Types: Using the Enneagram for Self-Discovery*]

The inner landscape of the nine resembles someone riding a bicycle on a beautiful day, enjoying everything about the flow of the experience. The whole picture, the entire situation is what is pleasant and identified with, rather than any particular part. The inner world of nines is this experience of effortless oneness. Their sense of self comes from being in union with the other.

Nines are open and optimistic. Nines are the primary personality type in the relating triad (see Figure 1, above). Although extraordinarily peaceful, they are also paradoxically vital and alive, in touch with their thoughts, feelings and desires. Very healthy nines are aware of even their aggressive feeling without being alarmed by them. They realize that having aggressions is not the same as acting aggressively or being destructive toward others. Self-respecting, they have enormous dignity because they are aware of their true worth, without the faintest whiff of egocentricity or self-congratulation.

They are fully present as individuals, and because they can see themselves as they really are, they can see others as they really are. Very healthy nines are firmly in their own center, enormously capable of dealing with problems because of the deep inner unity they have achieved. They actively inhabit their own consciousness, as it were. It is an extremely private, almost spiritual event, difficult to observe directly, or describe. At their best, very healthy nines are an example to all the personality types of what it means to be at one with the self and at one with the world.

They are an example of the profound unity that is possible for human beings. They contain a self-possession and a self-surrender so profound as to have mystical overtones. They are so effortlessly themselves, and so completely receptive, that very healthy nines must reflect what human beings were like before the fall into self-consciousness and alienation. They are a living reminder that, when all is said and done, we are each a gift to the other, just as the other is a gift to us.

The Receptive Person

Nines are able to identify with others, giving themselves to those who are central to their lives. They are extraordinarily receptive, capable of identifying with others, so completely that, for better or for worse, they are not self-aware, introspective or self-doubting. Nines have a great capacity for loving and sustaining others, since they are so unselfconsciously accepting, there are few conflicts in their emotional lives or in their relationships. Nines see themselves as peaceful. They have a high tolerance for stress and irritation. They are patient, imperturbable, relaxed, and tranquil.

Where do we look in Rosa Parks' life for indications of the characteristics of the nine? The book *Quiet Strength* is a good source, as are the various works on Rosa Parks, including: *Rosa Parks: The Movement Organizes*, by Kai Friese; *The Montgomery Bus Boycott*, by R. Conrad Stein; and Rosa Parks and the Montgomery Bus Boycott by Teresa Celsi.

The first trait we look to is the peaceful serenity of Rosa Parks, the deep inner unity. When arrested for refusing to budge from her seat on a Montgomery city bus on December 1, 1955, she showed no fear. In his book, *The Montgomery Bus Boycott*, Friese states on page 56,

"She wasn't afraid and she didn't get excited about anything," said E.D. Nixon, the President of the Montgomery Branch of the NAACP at the time."

There was, to be sure, a certain element of danger associated with her action. There was the chance that white reactionaries would harm her. When confronted with this reality, Mrs. Parks said:

"If you think it will mean something to Montgomery, and will do some good, I'll go along with it..."

She said this even in the face of potential physical harm. How did she get through with this? We will argue that it was her inner peace that got her through this. It was a deep faith in the Lord, a deep tranquility that could hold its head high in the face of adversity; and was not afraid to do what was right, even though the threats of bodily harm were there. In short, it was the characteristic of a healthy nine.

There is another aspect of the nine that comes out at this time. That is the example that Rosa Parks set for everybody. Because of her deep tranquility, she could be an example to others. And, in fact she said that is one of the greatest things she could give.

Clearly, Rosa Parks is serving as an example and thinks that living her life above reproach and as an example to others is the way to live. And it was this quality that made E.D. Nixon believe that Rosa Parks' case would make an excellent trial case the repressive Jim Crow bus segregation law.

Rosa Parks' case was to be the test case. There had been another test case earlier, but the girl involved had been pregnant and was not married, and so E.D. Nixon thought it best to drop the case. However, Rosa Parks, because of her ability to set an example for others (as a healthy nine), could serve as the trial case for the Montgomery segregationist bus law. So Rosa Parks was the person who was needed in this hour, because it took courage to stand up to the harsh law, but more important, to set the example to stand up to the harsh tide of events to come.

Another aspect of the nine is the ability to identify with others. One of Rosa's great moments in life came when she married Raymond Parks, at the age of eighteen in Montgomery. She and her husband built a life, and were, by all accounts happy together. Hers was a successful marriage, for she was able to identify and to coexist with her husband in peace and tranquility and harmony. Her marriage, like her life was a successful one, although the tide of events that was to wash over her was to bring a great deal of strain to the marriage.

However, nines are able to handle a great deal of stress and strain because of their serenity. And there would be stress during this time. The whites threw bombs; they threatened her. They shot guns, and threatened the black community, misguided as they were by blind prejudice. And through all of this upheaval, Rosa Parks followed in the steps of Martin Luther King and refused to lose her self-control and her center, which was her faith. The Montgomery Bus Boycott worked because the African-American community in Montgomery found in Rosa Parks someone they could stand behind, because of her example of humility and a life that was above reproach.

Nine with a One Wing

Rosa Parks is not uni-dimensional. She exhibits more than the traits of a healthy nine. It seems quite plausible that she has a "one-wing" in the Enneagram system. Rosa Parks is a nine with a one-wing.

The traits of the nine and those of the one tend to reinforce each other. In this subtype, we see people who are emotionally controlled and cool, although they may well display moments of anger and moral indignation. Healthy persons of this subtype possess enormous integrity and are extremely principled. Their great common sense helps them to be wise in their judgments, particularly about others. They are alert to issues of fairness and objectivity when they are called on to act or to judge situations.

The one-wing adds a thinking component to this subtype, balancing the nine's unselfconscious, receptive orientation. They enjoy teaching and may be moral leaders, teaching most effectively by their example. The nine's openness is combined with the one's objectivity. The result is simplicity and guilelessness towards others: peacefulness and moderation towards themselves.

Persons of this subtype might be crusaders of some sort because they have an idealistic streak that makes them want to improve the world in whatever ways they can. People of this subtype tend to be orderly and self-controlled. They can also be quite busy organizing the environment, or planning its organization by others, while maintaining the emotional disconnectedness characteristic of average nines.

This seems to sum up Rosa Parks—somewhat. It helps to explain one of her rare recorded outbursts, as recorded by a minister from Tennessee, who heard Rosa Parks speak in Montgomery one day. Rosa Parks and Martin Luther King Jr. were both in the Relating or body triad, where its all about managing the underlying instinctual anger.

"*She seemed fiery as she talked about the billboards along the highway [call-ing King a communist]. Later, the minister told a congregation of Rosa Parks words: 'My life has been hard: As a small girl, I had to run-or thought I had to-from the Ku Klux Klan to escape being killed. My father was cheated out of his land by a white man. I did not get much education. I could not register to vote. I always worked hard for very little. Without education, and without being able to vote, I tried to be a good citizen. I did attend a workshop at the Highlander School, and I want to tell you that the only reason I don't hate every white man alive is Highlander and Myles Horton*" *(Friese, pg. 108).*

Here we have the outburst; the moral indignation that is characteristic of the nine with a one-wing. It was this moral indignation that fueled Rosa Parks' determination to do something about the situation of African Americans in the white man's world. Rosa Parks does have a bit of the crusader about her. She is an organizer: She worked in Congressman John Conyers' office beginning in 1965.

Although she had a great deal to be angry for, it is to her credit that she never let that anger erupt into violence. And she had good reason to be angry. The stresses and strains of the boycott put a strain on her marriage, and caused her poor husband to suffer a nervous breakdown. This is proof of the inner strain going on at this time. Only a person with the inner drive complemented by the deep serenity to persevere through all of this, could have pulled off what Rosa Parks did.

Thus, we are now able to project the Soul Path of growth, for all human types.

Type 1. Patience and self-control, overcoming anger and leading to Joy.

Type 2. Compassion overcoming pride, leading to Self-acceptance.

Type 3. Good works, overcoming deceit and hypocrisy, leading
       to Faith.

Type 4. Kindness, overcoming envy, leading to Patience.

Type 5. Gentleness, overcoming greed, leading to Endurance.

Type 6. Faith, overcoming anxiety, leading to Peace.

Type 7. Joy, overcoming gluttony, leading to Gentleness.

Type 8. Endurance, overcoming lust, leading to Compassion.

Type 9. Peace, overcoming sloth, leading to Good Works.

Conclusion

In 1988, she appeared at the Democratic National Convention in Atlanta, Georgia, with presidential candidate Jesse Jackson. Jesse Jackson said of her: "Rosa Parks: We all stand on her shoulders." She has been awarded the Medal of Freedom, the highest honor given to a citizen of the United States, and received numerous other awards and honors, all for a simple act of courage. She was the personality that was needed at a certain time and place, she authored a major chapter in civil rights history as a result.

And now, at this 50-year anniversary of the Montgomery Movement, it is surely the time that the Nobel Peace Prize must be awarded to her, under whatever conditions as are now possible. This is all our challenge the "we— as a people.

Chapter 12

Let's Save All Our Children

A National Kitchen Table Summit: From desperation, to jubilation!
An invitation and a summons: Your presence is required.

In spite of a perception that our American society never had it so good, there is a gnawing reality that reminds us, with countless agonizing tragedies of death at too early an age, both in the inner city and the outer cities of our land, that maybe we have never had it so bad as we do now. With major Columbine-High-School-type tragedies so long lasting in our memory, and as we gear up for each season, we must remind ourselves that we cannot, and we dare not go back to business as usual. Let's save all our children, the children of the rich, and the children of the poor!

The black church under King knew how to help the biblical as well as the contemporary character types, such as rich Zacchaeus, save their own grandchildren. Equally, King showed us how to save our own, the children of our churches and communities. This, we must relearn, and do it right away, and join together as a global world house family, in undertaking this major challenge.

To that end, our communities must undertake an urgent inquiry into healing the soul of our troubled society.

One way to frame the general question is: What are some key national and local strategies for healing the soul of a suffering society so that homes and schools can become beloved learning communities, and not incubators of inner city Jail Trails, or outer city death traps? Our children are crying, and we must find better answers, and right away. Let us lay aside our ordinary pursuits, and pursue what is now most real for all ofus.

This general question must be engaged, and rigorously embraced soon and very soon. It must be done through what Dr. Russ Quaglia, of the Global Center for Student Aspirations, defines as the need, not for a national White House, but a National Kitchen Table Summit, taking place in every home and school, in every parish, synagogue, and mosque, in the State House and the White House. As quietly as is kept, that was King's big secret. Then and now, the question we all would like to chew on together is: What do we want to be and become, as a family, a nation, or as a world house family?

Remember King at the kitchen table back in Montgomery, on that fateful night in December 1955, when fear tempted him to turn back from Rosa Parks' dream—and his own. That very week highlighted once again, the oppression felt daily by Montgomery, Alabama's Negro citizens. Mrs. Rosa Parks had just struck her blow for freedom—her own, and ours—although at that point, few people knew it. Mrs. Parks did! And the ball was passed to the new young preacher in town, named Rev. King.

What God had in mind for Montgomery—although even King is not remembered as having used the term—was a "grand jubilee." Back there, at that point, only the vision of jubilee existed in the mind and heart of God, and hints of it, in Mrs. Park's soul, otherwise, why would she have done such a daring thing, which conceivably could have cost her, her very life.

The sense of oppressiveness and desperation that fell over Montgomery, and the entire South at that time, was very much like the sense of chaos and oppressiveness that has settled, like a dark cloud, all over modem day America, and the world. Oppression can be caused by the hate or insensitivity of others, or it can be generated as a kind of selfhatred and self-oppression. And that seems like what has happened in America, what our late friend, Dr. James Melvin Washington called soul murder. He can now only pray about it and cheer us on from a higher balcony in glory, but we can complete the needed inquiry and the healing which must follow.

Meanwhile, back in Montgomery, God had ordained young Rev. King for this task of lifting this dark cloud of chaos hate and fear, and he would later call it, healing the soul of America. This was one of the most important assignments God would give King and his associates.

If King would keep faith with God's jubilee vision, God would give America its jubilee victory. In 1955, on a desolate night in December, when the forces of hate had gotten word that the Negroes were about to make their move for freedom, the devil got nervous, devil smart, and devil busy. The devil struck a blow for status quo, by attempting to plant fear, and then surrender before the battle, into the heart of King. King found himself at the kitchen table, stating his reluctance to God, and drowning his fears in pots of coffee. This was the Original Kitchen Table Summit. When King, after many hours of prayer, was able to pray like his master leader, Jesus, "Not my will, but Thy will be done," the oppressive clouds of fear and chaos were lifted from his soul, and he told God, "Here Am I, send me." The rest is history-that is, God's jubilee Story-with King and Mrs. Parks leading a cast of major actors and actresses in God's jubilee drama, with an able cast of supporting players. I count myself among the early supporting cast, first in Lynchburg, Virginia, as president of the Lynchburg Improvement Association; an early affiliate of the Southern Christian Leadership Conference; and at age 28, one of the youngest members of King's Southern Christian Leadership Conference national board.

Now, here we all are some 50-plus years later, the nation-along with the world-finds itself in a panic mode. How can America celebrate when the clouds of oppressive chaos, fear, and hate hang so low, as to claim so many victims, from inner cities to suburbs, from nation to nation, family to family, and generation to generation? We need to pause, and hold a National Kitchen Table Summit, from the White House to your house; the school house to the work house; from the church (synagogue, mosque) house to the jailhouse; from the state house to the corporate house. Let every house that lives get the spirit, and go from jubilee vision, to jubilee victory, and see how good it feels!

That's when jubilee becomes as real as jubilation. We must do it now and we must do it together. Talk about dialogue on race, there must be more and it must become more than talk. Talk about a dialogue on families not making it, and feeling oppressed, by poor health, by soul sickness, by burdensome debt, by the very way they see themselves from day to day in their plight. Or talk about substance-abusing Generation X, and going from love-deprivation to love-saturation, love not seen in these parts lately.

They can come to see that a soul-high is higher than any other high. Or talk about families who are making it economically, yet finding themselves feeling oppressed and depressed in every other way. We cry out with the psalmist, "Why art Thou cast down, O my Soul, and why art thou disquieted within me? (*The Holy Bible, King James Version*)" We say with the old Negro spiritual (with a slight twist), "There is a balm in Gilead, to make the wounded soul, whole." Yes!

At a time of unusually high levels of wealth creation, the nation is feeling sick to its core, its soul reeling, and its mantle of leadership falling-is surely a time to hold a new jubilee summit, a National Kitchen Table Summit. It can involve character empowerment studies, in church, town, and gown. To that end, let the nation's universities, houses of worship, and the town halls of cities, suburbs, and counties, engage one another, face to face, and technology by technology, until we go from desperation to jubilation.

A 40-day trial period, (from January 15 to February 14—a first cycle) could build up a repertoire of insights as to where we then go with it. A kind of church, town, and gown exercise is the only promising way ahead for the nation at this critical point in its history. That first cycle—beginning on Martin Luther King's birthday—comes to a 40-day majestic closure, on Valentine's Day.

Several major new resources are now available, to aid this dialogue. The first is a major new work, The Wisdom of the Enneagram, by two of the world's foremost writers and teachers of the Enneagram, Don Richard Riso, and Russ Hudson. It is now available at your local bookstore. A second resource, which encapsulates that summit as a religious experience for African Americans, is the Jubilee Bible, published and already released, by the American Bible. And finally, Worldwide Laws of Life, 200 Eternal Spiritual Principles, by John Marks Templeton, (Radnor, PA: Templeton Foundation Press, 1997), is a must. Also by Templeton, Agape Love will help cement ties between the many faith communities and practitioners.

In this truly new, national dialogue, we will figure out together, what are the steps to go from desperation to jubilation, and we will set the stage in America and the world, for a joyful and jubilant new day. A daily discussion at the kitchen table of all those willing to be part of breathing new life into an old dream—the American dream—would involve individual families in a discussion of how to discern the presence or absence of love in their own family and how they might learn to maximize their well-being as a family within the whole world house family.

Surely, such rich dialogue, earnestly being engaged in families across the globe, offers great promise for the renewal of hope, and the prospect of love in communities everywhere, issuing forth into a grand beloved economy for all. It's a dream we cannot live without!

Part One:
Faith Beyond Doubt

"Can these bones live?" Ezekiel 37:3a

Chapter 13

The Jubilee-Grounded Congregation

Congregations that desire to implement a Martin Luther King, jubilee-based initiative-whether Christian, Jewish, or Muslim-will find useful direction here.

Background

In modem society, the word "jubilee" strikes a quaint sound with few known historical connections. Most Americans will likely be surprised to learn that the jubilee scripture, Leviticus 25:10, is inscribed on the Liberty Bell, or that the British and American legal systems of bankruptcy laws come out of the jubilee tradition. Also, the university system of the sabbatical for its favored professors comes out of the jubilee model. Moreover, Maria Augusta Neal envisioned the day when the nation would institute a sabbatical year for all its workers, in her book titled, *The Theology of Relinquishment* (1968). Surely, an idea whose time has come.

Joseph Donders (1985) informs us that the Gabbra are a nomadic people in the Northeast of Kenya. "They live in one of the driest areas of East Africa. In 1981, they celebrated their year of jubilee, ending another cycle of fifty years in their existence. In the year of jubilee crooked affairs are straightened out, injustice is righted, debts are settled, cattle (the only property) are re-allotted and sins are forgiven. This is not a myth; it is a story; it is not an ideal that they believe should be fulfilled. It really happened in 1981 after a year of preparation."

The story of jubilee is well established in both the Old and the New Testaments, although the record of its practice is barely known. Most African Americans are oblivious to the fact that it was their slave forebearer's growing love for the Bible, which most of them could not even read, but from which they culled certain core beliefs, among which jubilee was prominent.

When one examines their collective activity immediately following Emancipation in 1865, it becomes abundantly clear that those same slave fore-bearers created within their first 50 years after slavery, the institutional framework of family, black churches, black colleges, black press, and black businesses by which that community has survived to the present time. One would be hard-pressed to ignore their understanding and love for jubilee. It was a main ingredient in their push for advancement.

The church properly begins its study and examination of the jubilee with our Lord, as recorded in Luke 4:16-30. It is well known as that section of scripture, which begins, "the spirit of the Lord is upon me, Because He has anointed me to preach the gospel to the poor" (King James Version). After finishing the reading, he sat down, and said to them, "Today this scripture is fulfilled in your hearing" (verse 21). There were six provisions set forth: (1) he had been anointed to preach the gospel to the poor, (2) sent to heal the broken-hearted, (3) sent to proclaim liberty to the captives, (4) recovery of sight to the blind, (5) to set at liberty those who are oppressed, and (6) to proclaim the acceptable year of the Lord.

This rendition in Luke differs in a few slight details from the passage in Isaiah 61, which our Lord read, on that day. Luke adds provision four above, "recovery of sight to the blind." Provision five of Luke 4 in Isaiah 61 becomes, "and the opening of the prison to those who are bound."

The original text is from Leviticus 25:10, "And you shall consecrate the fiftieth year, and proclaim liberty throughout all the land to all its inhabitants. It shall be a jubilee for you; and each of you shall return to his possession, and each of you shall return to his family." It focuses on provisions related to land use, redemption of lost land, pricing and selling considerations in relation to jubilee guidelines, and the injunction that "you shall not oppress one another" (verse 17). This text differs from the former two, in that it explicitly states that "the acceptable year of the Lord" (Luke 4:19 and

Isaiah 61 :2a) is in fact "the year of jubilee."

Once having announced this as his central mission, Jesus illustrated how the jubilee would work, and extended the traditional boundaries of family-hood beyond the nation of Israel, to include foreigners in the provisions of God's jubilee, for all the nations of the earth.

Now flashing back to the Old Testament situation which the Leviticus account addressed, we discover that God was preparing the disparate tribal bands who yearned to become Israel, the nation of God's original promise to Abraham, on how to move from a nomadic existence to a people of set-tlement (25 :2), with viability and endurance. There were core beliefs tied into a set of institutions, which must be observed, if the people of promise were to become the nation of promise, with their own land of promise. While in the Leviticus account these provisions were to be kept within the Hebrew blood nation, Jesus expanded familyhood to all the nations, the one-blood nation.

In the Leviticus account, the jubilee-the fiftieth year (i.e., the year after the succession of seven sabbatical years) in which all the land alienated from its owners was to be returned to the families of those to whom it had been originally allotted, and all bondsmen of Hebrew blood were to be liberated.

As the church moves to recapture its knowledge and understanding of the biblical jubilee, certain things will stand out from the start. First, the jubilee is always associated with the activity and presence of God's Spirit, as explicitly stated in the Isaiah 61 and Luke 4 accounts. In the Leviticus ac-count, it is represented as the Lord speaking directly to Moses. The church will yield abundant fruitfulness of jubilee wisdom as it undertakes its exam-ination and study of the biblical jubilee under the consistent surrender to God's Holy Spirit.

Second, one will find the provisions of jubilee as enduring objectives and outcomes in the life, ministry, and work of Jesus, especially following his announcement of jubilee and its fulfillment in himself, at the home town synagogue. Thirdly, the whole death and Resurrection of Jesus was itself a major jubilee death and rebirth cycle. Then the new band of his followers, first the twelve, then the one-hundred and twenty, then the three-thousand began committing themselves to these core beliefs by the day of Pentecost, just fifty days following Easter.

It is interesting that the old cycle of 50 years is now matched to the new cycle of fifty days. In a sense, we find the first significant manifestation of the jubilee in the life of the new community, as recorded in Acts of the Apostles. Essentially, it recorded how they had shaped and were shaped around certain core elements. This is especially true with respect to Acts 4:32, their first stab at a kind of beloved economy. It was these scriptures which Karl Marx read and misunderstood; and, from that misunderstanding, plunged the world into a 75-year untruth.

Maria Harris offers significant insight into the first century church in discussing the broad curriculum which they embraced, and which we the current church of the whole, will find profit in engaging. (*Fashion Me A People*, 1989). She stated, in showing the history of its development:

> "*Rather, it is a reiteration and a reincorporating of the first curriculum of the Christian people, stated in Acts 2:32, 42-47. This Jesus God raised up, and of that, we are all witnesses, (kerygma)*
>
> *... And they devoted themselves to the apostles' teaching (didache;kerygma) and fellowship (koinonia),*
>
> *to the breaking of bread and prayers (leiturgia)*
>
> *... and all who believed were together and had all things in common (koinonia);*
>
> *and they sold their possessions and goods and distributed them to all, as any had need (diakonia).*"

These five elements will indeed form the core around which the church will find its way back to and through the biblical jubilee. In the five elements of its total life,

"Kerygma" is its curriculum for proclamation;

"Didache," its curriculum for teaching;

"Leiturgia," its curriculum for prayer;

"Koinonia," its curriculum for community;

"Diakonia," its curriculum for service

These five elements round out the full shape of the healthy and growing church, whether one church, or the church of the whole humanity. In its engagement with the study of the biblical jubilee, all five elements will be required for healthy and growing churches and communities.

Finally, it must be said that when it is ready for its jubilee pilgrimage, the church will move beyond every wall of religious separation and undertake this journey where ever possible, beseeching and welcoming our brothers and sisters of world Judaism and world Islam, and any other faith communities, to share in this conversation. The black church is seeking the kingdom in the midst of our chaos and pain, and invites others who long for the jubilee Beloved Community that our ancestors worked and prayed for, to come and go with us together on this journey.

It is most likely that as this occurs, we will together make discovery after joyful discovery, which we cannot even imagine at this point, and will find every wonder true.

Let it be remembered that one major slant on understanding our life together, our history as the people of America, has been the continuing need if less than constant commitment, "to define and refine our common understanding of the very idea and fact of liberty." (James MacGregor Burns, 1991). It is also that which Jesus and the *Jubilee Bible* invite and require us to proclaim.

As a church, as a nation and a people of the whole, (... the whole polity, the whole family, the whole world house of humanity) we will remember to the profit of our selves and our common future, that jubilee is a universal mandate for a civil world, and the civil society. No jubilee, no justice. No

167

justice, no jubilee. No jubilee, no civility. To our peril, we will discover that "earth shall have her jubilee," and with our wholehearted participation, it will be a jubilee of justice, peace, security, and the kingdom of character.

Jubilee will not be denied. With our neglect, disdain, and irreverence, earth shall have a jubilee of judgment. Is the judgment indeed upon America and the world, environmental pollution, the plagues of diseases we can't seem to control, conflicts and hatreds we once thought obsolete, violence now domesticated and destructive, on a scale unmatched at home and abroad. And this neglect of jubilee is especially hard on our youth, who seem to mirror most acutely, this "soul murder " against which the late James Melvin Washington warned us all us.

Those who have taken the trouble to find out know that jubilee is the guarantor of the good society, with its provisions for the self-adjudication of every kind of injustice and hostility that builds up in individuals, families, and societies over time.

It has been said that jubilee cannot work. It can be said that whether jubilee can work or not, we don't know; we haven't tried it, with intentionality or consistency of heart, mind, body or soul.

It must be said that a people of promise-coming into a land of promise, having in hand the book of promise-can do no better than studying that wisdom and earnestly praying their God to show them the way, whose delight is in giving them the love, the grace, and the courage to work and keep faith in God's promise of a new jubilee future.

A Collection of Speeches and Essays

The following is a collection of speeches delivered by some of the foreruners of the Beloved community... and yours truly.

"His spirit gives us breath, and we live again."
Ezekiel 37:14a

VIRGIL WOOD

This address was given by Dr. Benjamin Mays at my invitation, while I was dean and director of the African-American Institute of Northeastern University, in Boston, in 1982.

Meeting Tomorrow's Challenges Today with Academic, Moral, and Spiritual Preparation

by Benjamin E. Mays

People can be academically competent and yet completely lacking in morality and spiritual preparation. History is replete with such characters. And yet, such, characters may go far in leading the nation, the state, the city, and even the world in the wrong direction.

In the early Christian era, when emperors insisted on being worshipped as gods, Christians preferred to die rather than prove false to the Christian god. In order to strike back at the Christians, Nero set fire to the city and blamed it on the Christians. The Christians were persecuted under Domitian. Tradition has it that all the disciples died as martyrsexcept Judas-and one scripture says he committed suicide. Christ was crucified. The emperors at the time Christ was born did brutal, immoral things. For example, Herod the Great murdered Marianne, his wife, her two sons, her brother, her grandfather, and her mother. He had eight other wives and had children by six of them.

As indicated above, history has branded the Roman Emperor Nero with the reputation of being a monster of cruelty and has also credited him with the burning of Rome and the first persecution of the Christians. His appalling family background, stained as it was with incest and murder, no doubt, accounted for his instability of character. This displayed itself in the unbounded vanity that caused him to nurse artistic and histrionic pretensions that seriously undermined his imperial dignity and helped to bring about his early death and, with it, the extinction of the Julio-Claudian line descended from Julius Caesar. He became the first boy emperor at seventeen years of age.

Napoleon divorced Josephine because she bore him no children, and on April 2, 1810, he was married to the Archduchess Marie Louisa of Austria. The fruit of this union was a son. It was a most unhappy marriage for Napoleon, as Maria Louisa proved both heartless and dissolute. Napoleon was a great warrior, but he died a prisoner of war on the island of St. Helena March 5, 1821 and was buried there. In 1840, his remains were transferred to Paris. Now he is one of France's great heroes. Your life doesn't have to be exemplary to be a hero nor a man of great character. The exemplary and the non-exemplary become heroes.

Several brutal British kings were beheaded. Ridley and Latimer were burned at the stake. Just before the torch was lighted, they were heard to exclaim: "We shall set a fire in England today that shall never be put out."

Savonarola died for the Christian cause in Florence. Germany was perhaps the best-educated nation in history. Yet under the leadership of Hitler, that nation killed six million Jews. A so-called "superior" race held slaves in the United States and segregated them and lynched them. These were well-trained men. But they had no morality, no spirituality.

Let us apply these principles to our contemporary life and apply it to black boys and girls in high schools, colleges and universities. We blacks must bring morality and spirituality to America. I doubt if the white community can. It seems to be characteristic of black people to help each other due to the suffering Negroes have endured for 344 years of slavery, segregation, denigration, brutality, lynching and mob rule. Slavery drew black people together. They had no rights their masters had to respect. The female's body belonged to the master. The masters often reared two sets of children, one by his white wife and one by his black concubine. This same master would rear slaves to replenish his slaves and would sell his own children away from their masters.

Given the situation, this is understandable because the Negro was not human; he was sold as property. Our founding fathers did not include the slaves in their thinking as being deserving of liberty, justice, and freedom. Despite Jefferson's words, "I tremble for my country when I remember that God is just," he did not free his slaves before he died. General Washington, first President of the United States, did not free his slaves before he died.

Patrick Henry, great orator, crying out "Give me liberty or give me death," did not mean blacks, for Virginia held slaves. Lincoln, the great emancipator, did not fight the Civil War to free slaves but to save the Union. He said, "I will save the Union with slaves or without slaves." You remember the emancipation proclamation. The slaves were freed only in those states that were in rebellion against the federal government and not in those that were not in the rebellion. In his debate with Douglass in Illinois, when Douglass was accusing Lincoln of running for the presidency to free the slaves, Lincoln said that he would send the Negroes back to Africa, but they would die in ten days. Under these conditions, Negroes sang spirituals in order to endure - singing "Steal Away to Jesus. I ain't got long to stay here. My Lord is calling me, He is calling me by the thunder, The trumpet sounds within my soul, I ain't got long to stay"; and "Were you there when they crucified my Lord?" The master interpreted this to mean the slaves were happy.

The white people lacking in morality and spirituality made their leaders heroes. African Americans made heroes out of Jefferson, Lincoln and Washington and other founders of the republic. Even today, however, America does not take into consideration their hero's attitude towards the black man. He can hate Negroes and still be honored by the federal and state governments. For example, it is a well-known fact J. Edgar Hoover hated Negroes. He certainly hated Martin Luther King, Jr.'s "guts" and called Martin the biggest liar he had ever known.

And yet, Congress immortalizes Hoover, a man without morality and spirituality, by building the most expensive structure ever erected in honor of an American citizen, placing him above presidents of the United States. One does not even have to be a moral or good man to be immortalized. Senator Russell of Georgia who had no love for Negroes, and who voted against all civil rights legislation in Congress, has under construction an extravagantly expensive building. I believe it is a federal building. These men will be held up as models in class for our young people to emulate.

Unfortunately, our government has not been overly concerned about helping the black communities. Nevertheless, the ex-slaves have been very generous in fighting and dying for the American community. Even before the republic was established, Negroes fought for freedom in a land that denied them freedom. Crispus Attucks was among the first to lay down his life for America's freedom.

In testimony to that fact, his statue stands in Boston on the grounds of the state capitol. Thousands of Negroes fought in that war. Negroes fought in the War of 1812. Carter Woodson, in his book The Negro in Our History, points out that "Negroes made a record for valor displayed in this struggle on land and sea. They fought bravely under Perry and MacDonough." One of the officers commenting on the valor of Negro soldiers cited a black by the name of Johnson, saying:

"When America has such stars, she has little to fear from the tyrants of the ocean." Andrew Jackson, Woodson points out, "Appealed to the Negroes in preparing for the battle of New Orleans." He said, "Through a mistaken policy, you have heretofore been deprived of a participation in the glorious struggle for national rights in which our country is engaged. This no longer shall exist."

"As sons of freedom, you are now called upon to defend our most inestimable blessing. As Americans, your country looks with confidence to her adopted children for a valorous support, as a faithful return for the advantages enjoyed under her mild and equitable government. As fathers, husbands and brothers, you are summoned to rally around the standard of the eagle, to defend all which is dear in existence."

Three months after this proclamation when the Battle of New Orleans had been successfully fought, Jackson could say:

To the men of color-soldiers! From the shores of Mobile, I collected you to arms; I invited you to share in the perils and to divide the glory of your white countrymen. I expected much from you; for I was not uninformed of those qualities which must render you so formidable to an invading foe. I knew that you could endure hunger and thirst, and all the hardships of war. I knew that you loved the land of your nativity, and that, like ourselves, you had to defend all that is most dear to man. But you surpass my hopes. I have found in you, united to these qualities, that noble enthusiasm which impels to great deeds.

soldiers! The President of the United States shall be informed of your conduct of the present occasion; and the voice of the representatives of the American nation shall applaud your valor, as your General now praises your ardor. The enemy is near. His sails cover the lakes. But the brave are united; and, if he finds us contending among ourselves, it will be for the prize of valor, and fame its noblest reward.

Negroes fought in the American Revolutionary War. They saved Teddy Roosevelt when they advanced with him up San Juan Hill, defeating the Spanish and allowing the annexation of Puerto Rico. We fought in the Civil War, a war fought to keep us in slavery. Even after the passage of the 13th Amendment freeing the slaves, the 14th making them citizens, and the 15th giving the ex-slaves the ballot, all three were swept aside when the union soldiers were withdrawn in 1877. The Hayes Tilden compromise turned the slaves over to the South for the South to treat as it saw fit. And from 1877 to 1910, the ex-slaves were in slavery again, saving lynching, mob rule, and segregation.

After the Second World War, things were worse because Negroes had been drafted from all the southern states to go to Europe to fight to make the world safe for democracy. These soldiers had been treated decently in Europe, especially in France. They were not inclined to continue to accept at home the treatment they received before going to Europe. So, President Wilson sent Dr. Russa R. Moton to Europe to tell our soldiers that things would not be better. Moton advised our soldiers to return home, settle down, and buy a home. However, the Negro soldiers could not be as they were. They had seen a new world and they were new men. The white South, in many ways, told our soldiers to pull off their uniform, cringe and kowtow as "Niggers" should. No wonder race riots broke out in several places, perhaps the worst being Chicago. All this is to say that our soldiers have fought for community in the United States and their bodies are buried in the tombs all over Europe, Africa, America, and Southeast Asia.

I return to the theme of community. What can we do to apply what Negro medics are doing in sickle cell anemia that can be transplanted to Negro life elsewhere? In the light of the statistics listed below, supplied by Dr. Louis Sullivan of the Morehouse Medical School, the life expectancy of Negroes and the health conditions of blacks should draw us together to keep black people from dying out in a century. All forces in the Negro community-business, church, education, and Negro professional-must join hands to do this job.

It is assumed that black medics and black medical schools will be more interested in the health plight of Negroes than will white physicians or white medical schools. Life expectancy for black males is 59 years; for white males, 66 years. Life expectancy for black females is 65 years; for white females, 72 years. Diseases peculiar to blacks, or with higher incidences among blacks, include sickle cell anemia 1/625 blacks -50,000 in U. S.; hypertension, iron deficiency anemia, diabetes mellitus, some forms of cancer, rheumatoid arthritis, and diseases of malnutrition.

If the black community and if the black medics do this, nobody else in the community will. White medics and white medical schools may help, but the black medical schools and black people must take the initiative. In this sense, we Negroes are a community.

Why should white people care if in the next century or two the black race is completely blotted out because of their affliction? The race problem could be resolved without dropping bombs. I am convinced if this were the white race in this predicament, the President of the United States would be working on it, all congressmen would be concerned, all business people in the United States would be spending their monies to alleviate the situation. Budgets balanced or not Congress would shell out the money.

This is the challenge for black people in the United States. Let me quote "The Bridge Builder":

An old man, going along highway
Came to chasm-deep and wide
When the old man crossed in the twilight dim,
He stopped to build a bridge.
A young man came along, said to him:
"Old Man, why do you build here in the
Twilight dim: You've crossed the
Chasm deep and wide; you will never
Again pass this way."
The old man said:
"Young man, there are youths who will
Come this way and they too must cross
In the twilight dim. Young man, I am
Building this bridge for them."

Unless black people in the United States arouse everybody in this country to the plight we are in, nobody else will. Let the story be told in every classroom, every church, every television station. Let us tell it on the mountain, over the hills and everywhere that this is our mission; and, ifwe do not tell it, nobody else will. This is our mission, building bridges for our unborn children to cross in the twilight dim, toiling upward in the night, while the lazy and indolent slumber and sleep. It is urgent. I close with this poem which expresses the urgency of our plight.

God's Minute

I have only just a minute,

Only sixty seconds in it,

Forced upon me - can't refuse it

Didn't seek it, didn't choose it,

But it's up to me to use it.

I must suffer ifI lose it,

Give account ifI abuse it.

Just a tiny little minute

But eternity is in it!

VIRGIL WOOD

The following essay was written by Henry Drummond, based on
I Corinthians, Chapter 13: the "love chapter."

The Greatest Thing in the World

By Henry Drummond

Everyone has asked himself the great question of antiquity as of the modem world. What is the summum bonum-the supreme good? You have life before you. Once only you can live it. What is the noblest object of desire, the supreme gift to covet?

We have been accustomed to be told that the greatest thing in the religious world is Faith. That great word has been the keynote for centuries of the popular religion; and we have easily learned to look upon it as the greatest thing in the world. Well, we are wrong. If we have been told that, we may miss the mark. I have taken you, in the chapter which I have just read, to Christianity at its source; and there we have seen, "The greatest of these is love." It is not an oversight; Paul was speaking of faith just a moment before. He says, "If I have all faith, so that I can remove mountains, and have not love, I am nothing." So far from forgetting, he deliberately contrasts them, "Now abideth faith, hope, love," and without a moment's hesitation, the decision falls. "The greatest of these is love."

And it is not prejudice. A man is apt to recommend to others his own strong point. Love was not Paul's strong point. The observing student can detect a beautiful tenderness growing and ripening all through his character as Paul gets old; but the hand that wrote, "The greatest of these is love," when we meet it first, is stained with blood.

Nor is this letter to the Corinthians peculiar in singling out love as the summum bonum. The masterpieces of Christianity are agreed about it. Peter says, "Above all things have fervent love among yourselves." Above all things. And John goes farther, "God is love." And you remember the profound remark which Paul makes elsewhere, "Love is the fulfilling of the law"? Did you ever think what he meant by that? In those days men were working their passage to Heaven by keeping the Ten Commandments, and the hundred and ten other commandments which they had manufactured out of them.

Christ said, "I will show you a more simple way." If you do one thing, you will do these hundred and ten things, without ever thinking about them. If you love, you will unconsciously fulfill the whole law. And you can readily see for yourselves how that must be so. Take any of the commandments. "Thou shalt have no other gods before me." If a man love God, you will not require to tell him that. Love is the fulfilling of that law. "Take not His name in vain." Would he ever dream of taking his name in vain if he loved him? "Remember the Sabbath day to keep it holy."

Would he not be too glad to have one day in seven to dedicate more exclusively to the object of his affection? Love would fulfill all these laws regarding God. And so, if he loved man, you would never think of telling him to honour his father and mother. He could not do anything else. It would be preposterous to tell him not to kill. You could only insult him if you suggested that he should not steal-how could he steal from those he loved? It would be superfluous to beg him not to bear false witness against his neighbour. If he loved him, it would be the last thing he would do.

And you would never dream of urging him not to covet what his neighbours had. He would rather they possessed it than himself. In this way, "Love is the fulfilling of the law." It is the rule for fulfilling all rules, the new commandment for keeping all the old commandments, Christ's one secret of the Christian life.

Now Paul had learned that; and in this noble eulogy he has given us the most wonderful and original account extant of the summum bonum. We may divide it into three parts. In the beginning of the short chapter, we have love contrasted; in the heart of it, we have love analysed; towards the end, we have love defended as the supreme gift.

The Contrast

Paul begins by contrasting love with other things that men in those days thought much of, I shall not attempt to go over those things in detail. Their inferiority is already obvious.

He contrasts it with eloquence. And what a noble gift it is, the power of playing upon the souls and wills of men, and rousing them to lofty purposes and holy deeds! Paul says, "If I speak with the tongues of men and of angels, and have not love, I am become as sounding brass, or a tinkling cymbal." And we all know why. We have all felt the brazenness of words without emotion, the hollowness, the unaccountable unpersuasiveness, of eloquence behind which lies no love.

He contrasts it with prophecy. He contrasts it with mysteries. He contrasts it with faith. He contrasts it with charity. Why is love greater than faith? Because the end is greater than the means. And why is it greater than charity? Because the whole is greater than the part, love is greater than faith, because the end is greater than the means. What is the use of having faith? It is to connect the soul with God. And what is the object of connecting man with God? That he may become like God. But God is love. Hence faith, the means, is in order to love, the end.

Love, therefore, obviously is greater than faith. It is greater than charity, again, because the whole is greater than a part. Charity is only a little bit of love, one of the innumerable avenues of love, and there may even be, and there is, a great deal of charity without love. It is a very easy thing to toss a copper to a beggar in the street; it is generally an easier thing than not to do it. Yet love is just as often in the withholding.

We purchase relief from the sympathetic feelings roused by the spectacle of misery, at the copper's cost. It is too cheap-too cheap for us, and often too dear for the beggar. Ifwe really loved him, we would either do more for him or less.

Then Paul contrasts it with sacrifice and martyrdom. And I beg the little band of would-be missionaries-and I have the honour to call some of you by this name for the first time-to remember that though you give your bodies to be burned, and have not love, it profits nothing-nothing! You can take nothing greater to the heathen world than the impress and reflection of the love of God upon your own character. That is the universal language. It will take you years to speak in Chinese, or in the dialects of India.

From the day you land, that language of love, understood by all, will be pouring forth its unconscious eloquence. It is the man who is the missionary, it is not his words. His character is his message. In the heart of Africa, among the great Lakes, I have come across black men and women who remembered the only white man they ever saw before-David Livingstone; and as you cross his footsteps in that Dark Continent, men's faces light up as they speak of the kind doctor who passed there years ago. They could not understand him; but they felt the love that beat in his heart.

Take into your new sphere of labour, where you also mean to lay down your life that simple charm and your lifework must succeed. You can take nothing greater; you need take nothing less. It is not worthwhile going if you take anything less. You may take every accomplishment; you may be braced for every sacrifice; but if you give your body to be burned, and have not love, it will profit you and the cause of Christ nothing.

The Analysis

After contrasting love with these things, Paul in three verses, very short, gives us an amazing analysis of what this supreme thing is. I ask you to look at it. It is a compound thing, he tells us. It is like light. As you have seen a man of science take a beam of light and pass it through a crystal prism-as you have seen it come out on the other side of the prism broken up into its component color red and blue, and yellow, and violet, and orange, and all the colors of the rainbow-so Paul passes this thing, love, through the magnificent prism of his inspired intellect, and it comes out on the other side broken up into its elements. And in these few words we have what one might call the "spectrum of love," the analysis of love. Will you observe what its elements are? Will you notice that they have common names; that they are virtues which we hear about every day; that they are things which can be practiced by every man in every place in life; and how, by a multitude of small things and ordinary virtues, the supreme thing, the summum bonum, is made up?

The Spectrum of love has nine ingredients:

Patience	"Love sufferth long."
Kindess	"And is kind"
Generosity	"Love envieth not."
Humility	"Love Vaunteth not itself, is not puffed up."
Courtesy:	"Doth not behave itself unseemly."
Un-selfness:	"Seeketh not her own"
Good Temper:	"Is not easily provoked."
Guilelessness:	"Thinketh no evil."
Sincerity:	"Rejoiceth not in iniquity, but rejoiceth in truth."

Patience; kindness; generosity; humility; courtesy; unselfishness; good temper, guilelessness; sincerity these make up the supreme gift, the stature of the perfect man. You will observe that all are in relation to men, in relation to life, in relation to the known to-day and the near tomorrow, and not to the unknown eternity. We hear much of love to God; Christ spoke much of love to man. We make a great deal of peace with heaven; Christ made much of peace on earth. Religion is not a strange or added thing, but the inspiration of the secular life, the breathing of an eternal spirit through this temporal world. The supreme thing, in short, is not a thing at all, but the giving of a further finish to the multitudinous words and acts which make up the sum of every common day.

There is no time to do more than make a passing note upon each of these ingredients. Love is patience. This is the normal attitude of love; love passive, love waiting to begin; not in a hurry; calm; ready to do its work when the summons comes but meantime wearing the ornament of a meek and quiet spirit. Love suffers long; beareth all things; believeth all things; hopeth all things. For love understands, and therefore, waits.

Kindness ... love active. Have you ever noticed how much of Christ's life was spent in doing kind things-in merely doing kind things? Run over it with that in view, and you will find that He spent a great proportion of His time simply in making people happy, in doing good turns to people.

There is only one thing greater than happiness in the world, and that is holiness; and it is not in our keeping; but what God has put in our power is the happiness of those about us, and that is largely to be secured by our being kind to them.

"The greatest thing," says some one, "a man can do for his Heavenly Father is to be kind to some of His other children." I wonder why it is that we are not all kinder than we are. How much the world needs it. How easily it is done. How instantaneously it acts. How infallibly it is remembered. How superabundantly it pays itself back-for there is no debtor in the world so honourable, so superbly honourable, as love. "Love never faileth! Love is success, love is happiness, love is life. "Love," I say with Browning, "is energy of Life."

> For life, with all it yields of joy and woe
> And hope and fear,
> Is just our chance of the prize of learning love
> How love might be, hath been indeed, and is.

Where love is, God is. He that dwelleth in love dwelleth in God. God is love. Therefore, love ... without distinction, without calculation, without procrastination, love. Lavish it upon the poor, where it is very easy; especially upon the rich, who often need it most; most of all upon your equals, where it is very difficult, and for whom perhaps we each do least of all.

There is a difference between trying to please and giving pleasure. Give pleasure. Lose no chance of giving pleasure. For that is the ceaseless and anonymous triumph of a truly loving spirit. "I will pass through this world but once. Any good thing therefore that I can do, or any kindness that I can show to any human being, let me do it now. Let me not defer it or neglect it, for I shall not pass this way again."

Generosity ... "Love envieth not." This is love in competition with others. Whenever you attempt a good work, you will find other men doing the same kind of work, and probably doing it better. Envy them not. Envy is a feeling of ill will to those who are in the same line as ourselves, a spirit of covetousness and detraction. How little Christian work even is a protection against un-Christian feeling. That most despicable of all the unworthy moods which cloud a Christian's soul assuredly waits for us on the threshold of every work, unless we are fortified with this grace of magnanimity. Only one thing truly needs the Christian envy, the large, rich, generous soul which "envieth not."

And then, after having learned all that you have to learn this further thing, Humility-to put a seal upon your lips and forget what you have done. After you have been kind, after love has stolen forth into the world and done its beautiful work, go back into the shade again and say nothing about it. Love hides even from itself. Love waives even self-satisfaction. "Love vaunteth not itself, is not puffed up."

The fifth ingredient is a somewhat strange one to find in this summum bonum: Courtesy. This is love in society, love in relation to etiquette. "Love doth not behave itself unseemly." Politeness has been defined as love in trifles. Courtesy is said to be love in little things. And the one secret of politeness is to love. Love cannot behave itself unseemly. You can put the most untutored person into the highest society, and if they have a reservoir of love in their heart, they will not behave themselves unseemly. They simply cannot do it. Carlyle said of Robert Burns that there was no truer gentleman in Europe than the ploughman-poet. It was because he loved everything the mouse, and the daisy, and all the things, great and small, that God had made. So, with this simple passport, he could mingle with any society, and enter courts and palaces from his little cottage on the banks of the Ayr. You know the meaning of the word "gentleman."

It means a gentle man-a man who does things gently, with love. And that is the whole art and mystery of it. The gentle man cannot in the nature of things do an ungentle, an ungentlemanly thing. The ungentle soul, the inconsiderate, unsympathetic nature cannot do anything else. "Love doth no behave itself unseemly."

Unselfishness ... "Love seeketh not her own." Observe: Seeketh not even that which is her own. In Britain, the Englishman is devoted, and rightly, to his rights. But there come times when a man may exercise even the higher right of giving up his rights. Yet Paul does not summon us to give up our rights. Love strikes much deeper. It would have us not seek them at all, ignore them, eliminate the personal element altogether from out calculations. It is not hard to give up our rights. They are often external. The difficult thing is to give up ourselves.

The more difficult thing still is not to seek things for ourselves at all. After we have sought them, bought them, won them, deserved them, we have taken the cream off them for ourselves already. Little cross then, perhaps, to give them up. But not to seek them, to look every man not on his own things, but on the things of others. "Seekest thou great things for thyself' said the prophet; "seek them not." Why? Because there is no greatness in things.

Things cannot be great. The only greatness is unselfish love. Even self-denial in itself is nothing, is almost a mistake. Only a great purpose or a mightier love can justify the waste. It is more difficult, I have said, not to seek our own at all, than, having sought it to give it up. I must take that back. It is only true of a partly selfish heart. Nothing is a hardship to love, and nothing is hard. I believe that Christ's yoke is easy. Christ's "yoke" is just His way of taking life. And I believe it is an easier way than any other. I believe it is a happier way than any other.

The most obvious lesson in Christ's teaching is that there is no happiness in having and getting anything, but only in giving. I repeat: there is no happiness in having, or in getting, but only in giving. And half the world is on the wrong scent in the pursuit of happiness. They think it consists in having and getting, and in being served by others. It consists in giving and serving others. He that would be great among you, said Christ, let him serve. He that would be happy, let him remember that there is but one way. It is more blessed, it is more happy to give than to receive.

The next ingredient is a very remarkable one: good temper. "Love is not easily provoked." Nothing could be more striking than to find this here. We are inclined to look upon bad temper as a very harmless weakness. We speak of it as a mere infirmity of nature, a family failing, a matter of temperament, not a thing to take into very serious account in estimating a man's character. And yet here, right in the heart of this analysis of love, it finds a place; and the Bible again and again returns to condemn it as one of the most destructive elements in human nature.

The peculiarity of ill temper is that it is the vice of the virtuous. It is often the one blot on an otherwise noble character. You know men who are all but perfect and women who would be entirely perfect, but for an easily ruffled, quick-tempered or "touchy" disposition. This compatibility of ill temper with high moral character is one of the strangest and saddest problems of ethics. The truth is there are two great classes of sins-sins of the body, and sins of the disposition. The prodigal son may be taken as a type of the first, the elder brother of the second. Now society has no doubt whatever as to which of these is the worse. Its brands fall, without a challenge, upon the prodigal. But are we right?

We have no balance to weigh one another's sins, and coarser and finer are but human words; but faults in the higher nature may be less venial than those in the lower, and to the eye of Him who is love, a sin against love may seem a hundred times more base. No form of vice, not worldliness, not greed of gold, not drunkenness itself, does more to unChristian society than evil temper. For embittering life, for breaking up communities, for destroying the most sacred relationships, for devastating homes, for withering up men and women, for talking the bloom off childhood; in short, for sheer gratuitous misery-producing power, this influence stands alone.

Look at the elder brother, moral, hard-working, patient, dutiful-let him get all credit for his virtues-look at this man, this baby, sulking outside his own father's door. "He was angry," we read, "and would not go in." Look at the effect upon the father, upon the servants, upon the happiness of the guests. Judge of the effect upon the prodigal-and how many prodigals are kept out of the kingdom of God by the unlovely characters of those who profess to be inside?

Analyse, as a study in temper, the thundercloud itself as it gathers upon the elder brother's brow. What is it made of? Jealousy, anger, pride, uncharity, cruelty, self-righteousness, touchiness, doggedness, sullenness-these are the ingredients of this dark and loveless soul. In varying proportions, also, these are the ingredients of all ill temper. Judge if such sins of the disposition are not worse to live in, and for others to live with, than sins of the body. Did Christ indeed not answer the question Himself when He said, "I say unto you, that the publicans and the harlots go into the kingdom of heaven before you." There is really no place in heaven for a disposition like this.

A man with such a mood could only make heaven miserable for all the people in it. Except therefore, such a man be born again, he cannot, he simply cannot, enter the kingdom of heaven. For it is perfectly certain-and you will not misunderstand me-that to enter Heaven a man must take it with him.

You will see then why temper is significant. It is not in what it is alone, but in what it reveals. This is why I take the liberty now of speaking of it with such unusual plainness. It is a test for love, a symptom, a revelation of an unloving nature at bottom. It is the intermittent fever which bespeaks un-intermittent disease within; the occasional bubble escaping to the surface which betrays some rottenness underneath; a sample of the most hidden products of the soul dropped involuntarily when off one's guard,- in a word, the lightning form of a hundred hideous and un-Christian sins. For a want of patience, a want of kindness, a want of generosity, a want of courtesy, a want of unselfishness, are all instantaneously symbolised in one flash of temper.

Hence, it is not enough to deal with the temper. We must go to the source, and change the inmost nature, and the angry humours will die away of themselves. Souls are made sweet not by taking the acid fluids out, but by putting something in-a great love, a new spirit, the spirit of Christ. Christ, the spirit of Christ, interpenetrating ours, sweetens, purifies, transforms all. This only can eradicate what is wrong, work a chemical change, renovate and regenerate, and rehabilitate the inner man: Willpower does not change men. Time does not change men. Christ does.

Therefore, "Let that mind be in you which was also in Christ Jesus." Some of us have not much time to lose. Remember, once more, that this is a matter of life or death. I cannot help speaking urgently, for myself, for yourselves. "Who so shall offend one of these little ones, which believe in me, it were better for him that a millstone were hanged about his neck, and that he were drowned in the depth of the sea." That is to say, it is the deliberate verdict of the Lord Jesus that it is better not to live than not to love. It is better not to live than not to love.

Guilelessness and sincerity may be dismissed almost with a word. Guilelessness is the grace for suspicious people.

And the possession of it is the great secret of personal influence. You will find-if you think for a moment-that the people who influence you are people who believe in you. In an atmosphere of suspicion, men shrivel up; but in that atmosphere they expand and find encouragement and educative fellowship. It is a wonderful thing that here and there in this hard, uncharitable world there should still be left a few rare souls who think no evil. This is the great un-worldliness. Love "thinketh no evil," imputes no motive, sees the bright side, puts the best construction on every action. What a delightful state of mind to live in! What a stimulus and benediction even to meet with it for a day!

To be trusted is to be saved. And if we try to influence or elevate others, we shall soon see that success is in proportion to their belief of our belief in them. For the respect of another is the first restoration of the self-respect a man has lost; our ideal of what he is becomes to him the hope and pattern of what he may become.

"Love rejoiceth not in iniquity, but rejoiceth in the truth." I have called. This sincerity from the words rendered in the authorised version of the Bible by "rejoiceth in the truth." And, certainly, were this the real translation, nothing could be more just. For he who loves will love truth not less than men. He will rejoice in the truth rejoice not in what he has been taught to believe; not in this church's doctrine or in that; not in this ism or in that ism; but "in the truth." He will accept only what is real; he will strive to get at facts; he will search for truth with a humble and unbiased mind, and cherish whatever he finds at any sacrifice.

But the more literal translation of the revised version calls for just such a sacrifice for truth's sake here. For what Paul really meant is, as we there read, "Rejoiceth not in unrighteousness, but rejoiceth with the truth, a quality which probably no one English word-and certainly not Sincerity adequately defines. It includes, perhaps more strictly, the self-restraint, which refuses to make capital out of others' faults; the charity, which delights not in exposing the weakness of others, but "covereth all things"; the sincerity of purpose, which endeavours to see things as they are, and rejoices to find them better than suspicion feared or calumny denounced.

So much for the analysis of love. Now the business of our lives is to have these things fitted into our characters. That is the supreme work to which we need to address ourselves in this world, to learn love. Is life not full of opportunities for learning love? Every man and woman every day has a thousand of them. The world is not a playground; it is a schoolroom. Life is not a holiday, but an education. And the one eternal lesson for us all is how better we can love. What makes a man a good cricketer? Practice. What makes a man a good artist, a good sculptor, a good musician? Practice. What makes a man a good linguist, a good stenographer? Practice. What makes a man a good man? Practice. Nothing else. There is nothing capricious about religion. We do not get the soul in different ways, under different laws, from those in which we get the body and the mind. If a man does not exercise his arm, he develops no biceps muscle; and if a man does not exercise his soul, he acquires no muscle in his soul, no strength of character, no vigour of moral fibre, nor beauty of spiritual growth. Love is not a thing of enthusiastic emotion. It is a rich, strong, manly, vigorous expression of the whole round

Christian character the Christ-like nature in its fullest development And the constituents of this great character are only to be built up by ceaseless practice. What was Christ doing in the carpenter's shop? Practicing though perfect, we read that He learned obedience. He increased in wisdom and in favour with God and man. Do not quarrel therefore with your lot in life. Do not complain of its never ceasing cares, its petty environment, the vexations you have to stand, the small and sordid souls you have to live and work with.

Above all, do not resent temptation; do not be perplexed because it seems to thicken round you more and more, and ceases neither for effort nor for agony nor prayer. That is the practice which God appoints you; and it is having its work in making you patient, and humble, and generous, and unselfish, and kind, and courteous. Do not grudge the hand that is molding the still too shapeless image within you. It is growing more beautiful though you see it not, and every touch of temptation may add to its perfection. Therefore, keep in the midst of life.

Do not isolate yourself. Be among men, and among things, and among troubles, and difficulties, and obstacles. You remember Goethe's words: *Es bildet ein Talent sich in der Stile, Doch ein Character in dem Strom der Welt. "Talent develops itself m solitude; character in the stream of life."* Talent develops itself in solitude-the talent of prayer, of faith, of meditation, of seeing the unseen; character grows in the stream of the world's life. That chiefly is where men are to learn love.

How? Now, how? To make it easier, I have named a few of the elements of love. But these are only elements. Love itself can never be defined. Light is a something more than the sum of its ingredient glowing, dazzling, tremulous ether. And love is something more than all its elements palpitating, quivering, sensitive, living thing. By synthesis of all the colours, men can make whiteness, they cannot make light. By synthesis of all the virtues, men can make virtue. They cannot make love. How then are we to have this transcendent living whole conveyed into our souls? We brace our wills to secure it. We try to copy those who have it. We lay down rules about it. We watch. We pray. But these things alone will not bring love into our nature. Love is an effect. And only as we fulfill the right condition can we have the effect produced. Shall I tell you what the cause is?

If you turn to the revised version of the first epistle of John, you will find these words: "We love, because He first loved us." "We love," not "We love Him" That is the way the old Version has it, and it is quite wrong. "We love- because He first loved us." Look at that word "because." It is the cause of which I have spoken. "Because He first loved us," the effect follows that we love, we love Him, we love all men. We cannot help it. Because He loved us, we love, we love everybody. Our heart is slowly changed.

Contemplate the love of Christ, and you will love. Stand before that Mirror, reflect Christ's character, and you will be changed into the same image from tenderness to tenderness. There is no other way. You cannot love to order. You can only look at the lovely object, and fall in love with it, and grow into likeness to it. And so, look at this perfect character, this perfect life. Look at the great sacrifice as he laid down himself, all through life, and upon the cross of Calvary; and you must love him.

And loving him, you must become like him. Love begets love. It is a process of induction. Put a piece of iron in the presence of a magnetized body, and that piece of iron for a time becomes magnetized. It is charged with an attractive force in the mere presence of the original force, and as long as you leave the, two side by side, they are both magnets alike. Remain side by side with Him who loved us, and gave Himself for us, and you too will become a centre of power, a permanently attractive force; and like Him you will draw all men unto you, like Him you will be drawn unto all men. That is the inevitable effect of love. Any man who fulfils that cause must have that effect produced in him.

Try to give up the idea that religion comes to us by chance, or by mystery, or by caprice. It comes to us by natural law, or by super natural law, for all law is Divine. Edward Irving went to see a dying boy once, and when he entered the room he just put his hand on the sufferer's head, and said, "My boy, God loves you," and went away. And the boy started from his bed, and called out to the people in the house, "God loves me! God loves me!" It changed that boy.

The sense that God loved him overpowered him, melted him down, and began the creating of a new heart in him. And that is how the love of God melts down the unlovely heart in man, and begets in him the new creature, who is patient and humble and gentle and unselfish. And there is no other way to get it. There is no mystery about it. We love others, we love everybody, we love our enemies, because He first loved us.

Love as Defense

Now I have a closing sentence or two to add about Paul's reason for singling out love as the supreme possession. It is a very remarkable reason. In a single word, it is this it lasts. "Love" urges Paul, "never faileth." Then he begins again one of his marvelous lists of the great things of the day, and exposes them one by one. He runs over the things that men thought were going to last, and shows that they are all fleeting, temporary, passing away.

"Whether there be prophecies, they shall fail." It was the mother's ambition for her boy in those days that he should become a prophet for hundreds of years God had never spoken by means of any prophet, and at that time the prophet was greater than the king. Men waited wistfully for another messenger to come, and hung upon his lips when he appeared as upon the very voice of God. Paul says, "Whether there be prophecies they shall fail." This book is full of prophecies. One by one they have "failed"; that is, having been fulfilled their work is finished; they have nothing more to do now in the world except to feed a devout man's faith.

Then Paul talks about tongues. That was another thing that was greatly coveted. "Whether there be tongues, they shall cease." As we all know, many centuries have passed since tongues have been known in this world. They have ceased. Take it in any sense you like. Take it, for illustration merely, as languages in general-a sense which was not in Paul's mind at all, and which though it cannot give us the specific lesson will point the general truth.

Consider the words in which these chapters were written-Greek. It has gone. Take the Latin the other great tongue of those days. It ceased long ago. Look at the Indian language. It is ceasing. The language of Wales, of Ireland, of the Scottish Highlands is dying before our eyes. The most popular book in the English tongue at the present time, except the Bible, is one of Dickens's works, his Pickwick Papers. It is largely written in the language of London street-life; and experts assure us that in fifty years it will be unintelligible to the average English reader.

Then Paul goes farther, and with even greater boldness adds, "Whether there be knowledge, it shall vanish away." The wisdom of the ancients, where is it? It is wholly gone. A schoolboy today knows more than Sir Isaac Newton knew. His knowledge has vanished away. You put yesterday's paper in the fire. Its knowledge has vanished away. You buy the old editions of the great encyclopedias for a few pence. Their knowledge has vanished away. Look how the coach has been superseded by the use of steam. Look how electricity has superseded that, and swept a hundred almost new inventions into oblivion.

One of the greatest living authorities, Sir William Thomson, said the other day, "The steam engine is passing away." "Whether there be knowledge, it shall vanish away." At every workshop, you will see, in the back yard, a heap of old iron, a few wheels, a few levers, a few cranks, broken and eaten with rust. Twenty years ago, that was the pride of the city. Men flocked in from the country to see the great invention; now it is superseded, its day is done. And all the boasted science and philosophy of this day will soon be old. But yesterday, in the University of Edinburgh, the greatest figure in the faculty was Sir James Simpson, the discoverer of chloroform.

The other day, his successor and nephew, Professor Simpson, was asked by the librarian of the University to go to the library and pick out books on his subject that were no longer needed. And his reply to the librarian was this: "Take every text book that is more than ten years old, and put it down in the cellar." Sir James Simpson was a great authority only a few years ago: men came from all parts of the earth to consult him; and almost the whole teaching of that time is consigned by the science of to-day to oblivion. And in every branch of science it is the same. "Now we know in part. We see through a glass darkly."

Can you tell me anything that is going to last? Many things Paul did not condescend to name. He did not mention money, fortune, fame; but he picked out the great things of his time, the things the best men thought had something in them, and brushed them peremptorily aside. Paul had no charge against these things in themselves. All he said about them was that they would not last. They were great things, but not supreme things. They were things beyond them. What we are stretches past what we do, beyond what we possess. Many things that men denounce as sins are not sins; but they are temporary. And that is a favorite argument of the New Testament.

John says of the world, not that it is wrong, but simply that it "passeth away." There is a great deal in the world that is delightful and beautiful; there is a great deal in it that is great and engrossing; but it will not last. All that is in the world, the lust of the eye, the lust of the flesh, and the pride of life, are but for a little while. Love not the world therefore. Nothing that it contains is worth the life and consecration of an immortal soul. The immortal soul must give itself to something that is immortal. And the only immortal things are these: "Now abideth faith, hope, love, but the greatest of these is love."

Some think the time will come when two of these three things will also pass away-faith into sight, hope into fruition. Paul does not say so. We know but little now about the conditions of the life that is to come. But what is certain is that love must last. God, the eternal God, is love. Covet therefore that everlasting gift, that one thing which it is certain is going to stand, that one coinage which will be current in the universe when all the other coinages of all the nations of the world shall be useless and un-honoured. You will give yourselves to many things; give yourselves first to love. Hold things in their proportion. Hold things in their proportion. Let at least the first great object of our lives be to achieve the character defended in these words the character, and it is the character of Christ-which is built round love.

I have said this thing is eternal. Did you ever notice how continually John associates love and faith with eternal life? I was not told when I was a boy that "'God so loved the world that He gave His only begotten Son, that whosoever believeth in Him should have everlasting life." What I was told, I remember, was, that God so loved the world that, if I trusted in Him, I was to have a thing called peace, or I was to have rest, or I was to have joy, or I was to have safety. But I had to find out for myself that whosoever trusteth in Him-that is, whosoever loveth Him, for trust is only the avenue to love-hath everlasting life. The gospel offers a man life.

Never offer men a thimbleful of gospel. Do not offer them merely joy, or merely peace, or merely rest, or merely safety; tell them how Christ came to give men a more abundant life than they have, a life abundant in love, and therefore abundant in salvation for themselves, and large in enterprise for the alleviation and redemption of the world. Then only can the gospel take hold of the whole of a man, body, soul, and spirit, and give to each part of his nature its exercise and reward. Many of the current gospels are addressed only to a part of man's nature. They offer peace, not life; faith, not love; justification, not regeneration.

And men slip back again from such religion because it has never really held them. Their nature was not all in it. It offered no deeper and gladder life-current than the life that was lived before. Surely, it stands to reason that only a fuller love can compete with the love of the world.

To love abundantly is to live abundantly, and to love forever is to live forever. Hence, eternal life is inextricably bound up with love. We want to live forever for the same reason that we want to live tomorrow. Why do you want to live tomorrow? It is because there is some one who loves you, and whom you want to see tomorrow, and be with, and love back. There is no other reason why we should live on than that we love and are beloved. It is when a man has no one to love him that he commits suicide. So long as he has friends, those who love him and whom he loves, he will live. Because to live is to love. Be it but the love of a dog, it will keep him in life; but let that go and he has no contact with life, no reason to live. The "energy oflife" has failed.

Eternal life also is to know God, and God is love. This is Christ's own definition. Ponder it. "This is life eternal that they might know. Thee, the only true God, and Jesus Christ whom thou has sent." Love must be eternal. It is what God is. On the last analysis, then, love is Life. Love never faileth, and life never faileth, so long as there is love.

That is the philosophy of what Paul is showing us. The reason why in the nature of things love should be the supreme thing: because it is going to last; because in the nature of things it is an eternal life. That life is a thing that we are living now, not that we get when we die; that we shall have a poor chance of getting when we die unless we are living now. No worse fate can befall a man in this world than to live and grow old alone, unloving and unloved. To be lost is to live in an unregenerate condition, loveless and unloved; and to be saved is to love; and he that dwelleth in love dwelleth already in God. For God is love.

Now I have all but finished. How many of you will join me in reading this chapter once a week for the next three months? A man did that once and it changed his whole life. Will you do it? It is for the greatest thing in the world.

You might begin by reading it every day, especially the verses which describe the perfect character. "Love suffereth long, and is kind; love envieth not; love vaunteth not itself." Get these ingredients into your life. Then everything that you do is eternal. It is worth doing. It is worth giving time to. No man can become a saint in his sleep; and to fulfill the conditions required demands a certain amount of prayer and meditation and time, just as improvement in any direction, bodily or mental, requires preparation and care. Address yourself to that one thing; at any cost have this transcendent character exchanged for yours.

You will find as you look back upon your life that the moments that stand out, the moments when you have really lived, are the moments when you have done things in a spirit of love. As memory scans the past, above and beyond all transitory pleasures of life, there leap forward those supreme hours when you have been enabled to do unnoticed kindnesses to those around about you, things too trifling to speak about, but which you feel have entered into your eternal life.

I have seen almost all the beautiful things that God has made; I have enjoyed almost every pleasure that He has planned for man; and yet as I look back I see standing out above all the life that has gone four or five short experiences when the love of God reflected itself in some poor imitation, some small act of love of mine, and these seem to be things which alone of all one's life abide. Everything else in all our lives is transitory. Every other good is visionary. But the acts of love, which no man knows about, or can ever know about, they never fail.

In the book of Matthew, where the Judgment Day is depicted for us in the imagery of one seated upon a throne, and dividing the sheep from the goats, the test of a man is then not, "How have I believed?" but "How have I loved?" The test of religion, the final test of religion, is not religiousness, but love. I say the final test of religion at that great day is not religiousness, but love; not what I have done, not what I have believed, not what I have achieved, but how I have discharged the common charities of life. Sins of commission in that awful indictment are not even referred to. By what we have not done, by sins omission, we are judged.

It could not be otherwise. For the withholding oflove is the negation of the spirit of Christ, the proof that we never knew him, that for us he lived in vain. It means that he suggested nothing in all our thoughts, that he inspired nothing in all our lives that we were once near enough to him to be seized with the spell of his compassion for the world.

> "I lived for myself, I thought for myself,
> For myself, and none beside-
> Just as if Jesus had never lived,
> As if he had never died."

It is the son of man before whom the nations of the world shall be gathered. It is in the presence of humanity that we shall be charged. And the spectacle itself, the mere sight of it will silent judge each one. Those will be there whom we have met and helped; or there, the unpitied multitude whom we neglected or despised. No other witness need be summoned. No other charge than lovelessness shall be preferred. Be not deceived. The words which all of us shall one say hear, sound not of theology but of life, not of churches and saints but of the hungry and the poor, not of creeds and doctrines but of shelter and clothing, not of bibles and prayer-books but of cups of cold water in the name of Christ.

Thank God the Christianity of today is coming nearer the world's need. Live to help that on. Thank God men know better, by a hairsbreadth, what religion is, what God is, who Christ is, where Christ is. Who is Christ? He who fed the hungry, clothed the naked, visited the sick. And where is Christ? Where? Whoso shall receive a little child in my name receiveth me. And who are Christ's? Every one that loveth is born of God.

This sermon appeared in The African-American Pulpit," Judson Press: Valley Forge, Pa., Summer 1998.

How to Become Rich and Right! Luke 4:18; 19:8

By Virgil A. Wood

A people who are affluent and just will be a nation that is righteous and prosperous and worthy to be emulated, (a black and unknown bard... set apart).

A nation in which one percent of the people own wealth equal to that of the bottom 35 percent is a nation very much like Zacchaeus: treed up a tree. It has been reported in major newspapers across the nation that within the decade, the storehouse of old wealth will change hands to the tune of around ten trillion dollars. It is common knowledge that those holders of such enormous wealth are already consulting their army of advisors, and some have very wisely turned to their spiritual and faith advisors for sound advice on how to be rich and right. Everyone who is wealthy, or hopes to be, and wants to do it right will find guidance in reading Father John Haughey's splendid book *Virtue and Affluence: The Challenge of Wealth.*

It would be misleading for me to imply that money is a problem for the rich only. However, we are concerned in this message about those to whom much has been given. To the situation of the millionaires cited above, we would add the thought put forward by some that the average middle-class family today might well be on par with the wealthy of Jesus' day.

Based on the traditional teachings passed on by the church, it would appear that Jesus saw the predicament of the poor as being frozen in time. Didn't he once say that the poor would be with us always, perhaps issuing a proclamation of permanent condition, more than simply using a popular saying of the times? But it is clear from his teachings that Jesus viewed wealth as a critical potential problem for those who love it more than they love the God who is the source. This is the problem of the unrighteous mammon. When we look at this old problem in a new way, we discover that

Jesus had a great deal to say about wealth and, by implication, about those who are the "wealth wannabes."

The first lesson we receive from Jesus about the poor is in relationship to his own inaugural sermon in the hometown synagogue. In it we have a kind of guarantee to the poor of good news, right away: "He has anointed me to preach good news to the poor" (Luke 4:18, *The Holy Bible*, Revised Standard Version). Has this scripture been fulfilled in your hearing?

After carefully thinking through his purpose and mission, Jesus went home to announce to everybody in the hometown synagogue that he had been called to preach good news to the poor. When he showed up and told the poor, "Have I got some good news for all of you... ," they got excited and started following him around. When King showed up and announced good news for the poor, America was less merciful than Nazareth. They never gave him a chance to show what God wanted him to do about good news for the poor.

We glimpse the mind of Jesus concerning the wealthy by way of the story of the rich ruler who came seeking to find the answer to the good life, the life of salvation. The story of the rich ruler could be the plot for a play we might title rich, wrong, and miserable (Luke 18:18-30, Revised Standard Version). When Jesus analyzed this man's situation, he determined that the only way this person could be whole would require him to be separated from that which he loved more than all else. Go and sell all your possessions and give alms to the poor, Jesus admonished him.

Even Jesus' disciples remarked, "This is a hard saying." Who then can be saved? Jesus further opens up the riddle by saying, with humans, it is impossible; but with God, all things are possible-even opening the hearts of the wealthy. The ruler made his choice, but the situation is not exhausted with this story. We will find out more when we meet Zacchaeus.

The next story we have from Jesus illustrating the truth about the wealthy is the familiar story of the rich farmer who had just received a bumper crop and decided to tear down his smaller barns and build bigger ones in which to store (hoard) his goods. This could be the plot for a story titled "Rich, Wrong, and Dead " (Luke 12:16-21). Jesus makes clear that the destiny of those who hoard God's riches in barns and bank accounts, rather than in the hungry stomachs of poor folk-in the bins of kingdom business-court a similar fate and set themselves up for a life of misery and death.

We could ask, Why did Jesus counsel the rich ruler to give his all away and become penniless; pronounce the rich farmer a fool, losing his life and his soul; and yet approvingly declare Zacchaeus to be saved, becoming Mr. Rich and Right? Zacchaeus was a rich man up a tree, whom Jesus led to become Mr. Right.

This message asserts that Jesus made a promise on the first day of his preaching ministry, spent every waking moment fulfilling every promise with actual performance and results, and that his effectiveness with rich Zacchaeus was some of the best good news the poor folk in those parts had ever heard or witnessed. The transformation of Zacchaeus is one of the greatest stories of human transformation in all of the New Testament.

What we have here is a situation in which the friendship and love of Jesus effect a major bloodless revolution in that Zacchaeus offers reparations and restitution to those he had wronged economically as well as half of all his goods as alms to the poor. My guess is that after that settlement, there might be some question as to whether or not Zacchaeus had been reduced to poverty. But that is not the issue here. Jesus effects a major transformation in this very rich man's life, and Jesus never asked him for anything but lunch.

The new reality that Jesus brought about in the life of Zacchaeus and his neighbors stands in stark contrast to the facile acceptance the church makes of the status-quo situation of the poor in our nation at this time. My question to the church today is: What do you think, really, would be good news for poor people?

After all the explanations, nuances, and paralyses of analyses, what the poor really want is not to be poor anymore. It's that simple. They are the dispossessed who want back their land, the disinherited who want back their destiny, their options, their name, their crown, for themselves, their families, and all families. They want the option of developing themselves, their minds, their bodies, their souls, and then the right to the fruit of all their labors. It is the opposite of every kind of slavery, and they want it all. And Jesus promised it all to them: a life of abundance, both spiritual and material.

What Jesus offers the poor is spiritual wealth; economic wealth is often not far behind. The very notion of the eating of the body of Christ denotes a passing on of the ownership of God's creation to the whole people of God, "the body of Christ," which Paul said in 1 Corinthians 12:21-31 includes all God's children. In Acts 4, we find the brand-new post-Pentecost community establishing a new economic arrangement by which that community would order its life. In Acts 4:32 is recorded for all of posterity the spirit of love for economic relations that will be good and right for all times. So powerful was this vision of living that later on Karl Marx would read it, misunderstand its wisdom, and use it to terrorize the world for seventy-five years.

What Marx misunderstood and what Martin Luther King did understand is that this economic vision only works when based on love. It is a beloved economy. What the church has, misunderstood was that Jesus was serious about bringing economic and spiritual transformation to the poor and started it on the day of proclamation. The church has been even more reckless than Marx in many ways, particularly in its almost total disregard for this vision, this jubilee way of life, that was initially received by Moses (Leviticus 25); passed on by Trito-Isaiah (Isaiah 61); brought to life by Jesus (Luke 4:14-21); and later nurtured by Martin Luther King in his vision of a Poor People's Campaign.

To raise the issue of economic and spiritual development within the black church at this time-against the backdrop of recent major disappointments-is to run the risk of also stirring up further cynicism with respect to grand visions and dreams around a new economic future for black Americans.

On the one hand, it would seem that a whole generation might have to die off before such massive dreams could be entertained again. On the other hand, it may well be that this very predicament does in fact mandate that the whole church faces this issue head on and immediately.

Not only is the credibility of the black church very much affected, but also the very mission that we receive in Luke 4:14-21 from Jesus and that is reinforced by Martin King suggests that if the black church does not do it, and do it right, that it will not likely get done.

We have no choice but to reassess our situation, go back to the upper room for healing and direction, then get on with Pentecost and jubilee. We can do no less. And we must do it soon so that before the year 2007 it will already have become our new ritual of redemption.

To follow Jesus and Martin with respect to the poor, we must go to Zacchaeus's house and, with the strength to love even the wicked tax collector, pave a new highway of economic and spiritual redemption: Zacchaeus's statement after lunch was one of economic confession; Jesus' statement was one of spiritual salvation and transformation. He had indeed married the two, and in the process, Zacchaeus had become right and rich.

Someone must teach America that its true destiny is to be as just as it is affluent and to export into every nook and cranny of this world the economic and spiritual possibility raised by the very inclusion of the jubilee scripture on its liberty bell: "Proclaim liberty throughout all the land unto all the inhabitants thereof" (Leviticus 25:10, King James Version). Is this too grand a task for the faith communities, especially all those who are sons and daughters of father Abraham, who received the promise that his universal offspring would be as numerous as the sands of the sea?

The fact is that Jesus said more about money and economic matters than the church has been willing to accept or understand, much less teach and promulgate. The high level of economic illiteracy within the general population and especially among Christians is reprehensible, but redeemable. No public education that abandons our students to economic and moral illiteracy is complete. The great educational systems of the future will address both economic and moral objectives.

Our own church schools are fertile ground for both tasks, as indeed the first schools for freed slaves in our past struggles were the basements of caring congregations who knew that if they didn't do it, the job would not be done, or done with real effectiveness. In the New Testament, we have the framework for an appropriate theology of economic and spiritual practice, as set forth by our Lord in Luke-Acts. To the fine work many of our churches already do must now be added the task of economic literacy. Many in that select group of multimillionaires who met with Father Haughey for a number of weekend workshops surely, like Zacchaeus, found their way down out of the tree and found out what for them was the right thing to do, and many, no doubt, did it.

Poor folk in America who hear the words of Jesus in Luke 4:18 that the Spirit of the Lord ... has anointed me to proclaim good news to the poor have reason to wonder if the church really believes Jesus, if it ever did. It is clear that King believed Jesus, so investing his life in such a Poor People's Campaign that, in all likelihood, it cost him his life or the exchange of his life for the future of his and God's poor people. In a time when the ascent to political office is so well paved with wholesale demonizing of poor folk, a wider road of destruction has become the lot of the poor and with few, if any, significant advocates.

My prayer is that our brothers and sisters will take this not as any final word but merely as a discussion starter on how we together, all of us, can be thankful for whatever God has given us and then beseech God as to how we might best use our resources to create the Beloved Community with its beloved economy in our own time.

What I have attempted to set forth is a path over which we might travel after raising the initial question, Is there no permanent way out for the poor? When we are willing to be led by the same spirit, as was our Lord and consider the possibilities raised by his teachings, we will discover that the question mark has been straightened into an exclamation point. Yes, there is a way out for the poor and a way for the non-poor to establish the solidarity of human community, and in the process there is a way to set ourselves up for the unceasing flow of God's abundance to bless us all.

Those who have tried it have become our heroes. Notable among them is Oseola McCarty, who worked all her life as a laundry woman and gave her life savings of $150,000 to the University of Southern Mississippi in 1995 to establish a scholarship for needy AfricanAmerican students. She was quoted by Jet Magazine as saying, "I wanted to give some child the opportunity I didn't have. I hope this money can help children for years to come make their dreams come true." Subsequently, that initial gift had grown in the direction of a million dollars.

Surely Jesus would declare this the widow's mite a mighty big mite that has caused a whole nation to stop, think, and become more generous. Wasn't it Ms. McCarty's fore parents and ours who sang in the midst of their poverty:

> Let us break bread together on our knees;
> Let us break bread together on our knees.
> When I fall on my knees,
> With my face to the rising sun,
> O Lord, have mercy on me.

They had the sequence right. We must learn to break it, even as we learn to make it. Then an added verse might be:

> Let us make bread together on our feet;
> Let us make bread together on our feet.
> When we fall on our knees,
> With our face to the rising sun,
> O Lord, have mercy on us all. Amen.

An adaptation and "Blev'ers," as our awesome ancestors would say, "believers."

The Blev'ers' Jubilee - (When the love Comes)

1. Spread the Love, in the Blev'ers' Jubilee
Write my name on th' solid rock,
I been happy, since the Lord has set me free
I wannabe ready when th' Love comes.

2. Sign me up, for the Blev'ers' Jubilee,
Write my name on the roll,
I've been changed, since the Lord has set me free
I wannabe, ready, when th' Love comes.

3. Life me up, for the Blev' ers' Jubilee,
Plant my feet on th' solid Rock
My heart's been changed since I gave it to the Lord I wannabe,
ready, when th' Love comes.

4. Train me Lord for The Blev'ers' Jubilee,
Set my mind on your Love
I've been Free since the Lord's been teaching me
I wannabe, ready, when th' Love comes.

5. Send me Lord to The Blev'ers' Jubilee,
Stand by me on the line
My soul's so happy as I carry out your will
I wannabe, ready, when th' Love comes.

6. Bear our burdens through The Blev'ers' Jubilee,
Share the load with the Lord
We are rested as the truth has set us free
We, wannabe, ready, when Th' Love comes.

7. Bind our hearts, for The Blev'ers' Jubilee,
Fix them up for today
We will pray, rest, n' work, n' do our job
We, wannabe, ready, when Th' Love Comes.

To Be sung to the tune of "America the Beautiful"

Beloved Community
by Brother Virgil

1. Beloved Community, we're named and called by God
Humbl'n and pray'n, to seek God's face
Turning from our past wrongs,
America, America, forgiv'n and heal'd right now,
To dwell in peace, prosperity, is good for one and all.

2. **Beloved Community, King, Lincoln, Kennedy,**
And Johnson forged a nobler creed,
For one and all to be,
An American, an American,
Stand tall and reach the stars,
And let us every nation be,
And be for one and all.

3. Beloved America, red, white, black, yellow, brown
From every nation we have come
To live here now in peace,
America, America, god give us grace that we
Will find our true and nobler voice
For one humanity.

4. Beloved, Beloved, our country is for all,
Why can't we find a better way
To make it really so,
Beloved, Beloved, God mend thine every flaw,
Help us make up, and lift the ones
Who need a helping hand.

5. Beloved, Beloved, joy, peace, and love for all,
Patience, and kindness, long-suffering,
Faithfulness, self-control
Beloved, Beloved,
Goodness from one and all,
Till all the virtues from above
Are seen and felt below.

VIRGIL WOOD

Ms. Ledbetter, the keynote speaker for the 10th Annual Martin Luther King Scholarship Breakfast, gave this address to the Ministers Alliance of Rhode Island, of which the author was president, at the time. Used with permission of the speaker.

First Draft of a Black Contract with Beloved America
Beverly E. Ledbetter's, Esq.

On a recent trip, I happened to notice an insert inside a current issue of *National Geographic*. Although I only had time to glance at it, I was struck by the words which were purportedly carved on the walls of an ancient structure near Thebes. The inscription read: "Let us build, oh people." The story went on to tell how the ancient kings had engaged thousands of laborers in executing their grand design ...

This command, so common to ancient civilizations, resulted in exquisite structures, so masterfully constructed that they have withstood the ravages of time and nature for thousands of years. Visitors to these sights marvel at their size, their sumptuousness, and their imposing beauty.

Some have tried to calculate their workforce needed to erect them, others the method of their construction or the number of years needed to complete them. But few have wondered about the lives of those who toiled to make them a reality, for they were not kings, nor rulers nor leaders. Their lives and deeds were not recorded on the walls; their lives and deeds were the walls ...

It is a distinct honor to be with you today to share our memories of a different kind of King who also beseeched his people to build. But our King, Dr. Martin Luther King, Jr., was not interested in building magnificent physical structures. The work he envisioned for his people was quite different. When he used the phrase "Let us build," he had in mind a different kind of construction. And in remembrance of that King, we, the people, have embraced the call, the call to build something that would withstand the ravages of man, not time and nature, something that would symbolize the magnificence of the human heart, not the magnificence of the purse.

He laid the foundation for us with a dream of freedom and, using the tools of nonviolence, he showed us how to build a better and stronger America. His plans called for no intentional sacrifice of life or limb, but rather a sacrifice of our time, of our effort, and of our talent. The struggle for each is not to carve from mountains of stone the building blocks of temples or tombs, but rather to carve from hearts of stone the building blocks of humanity. Our job is not to lift granite walls into the air so hat buildings might stand with the clouds, but rather to life our voices to the sky so that our spirits might soar with the eagles. Our task is not to fill vast rooms with treasures and statues, but rather to fill the vastness of inhumanity with love and understanding. Our duty is not to preserve man for the eternal journey with balms, ointments, or salves, but rather to preserve humanity with the balm of equality, the ointment of opportunity, and the salve of justice.

Recalling the words of our new speaker of the House of Representatives (Newt Gingrich) that this is not just another day, and this is not just another Congress, we recognize that the nineties are not just another decade and we, the people, are not just another people.

We too want a contract with America—a contract with America to finish the building that Reverend King, the architect of a just society, laid the foundation for. A contract to complete a structure that would advance the cause of freedom and justice for all. The first draft of that contract was unveiled in December 1955 when Reverends King and Abertnathy addressed a packed audience of more than a thousand at Holt Street Baptist Church with an overflow crowd of another 5,000 standing outside and listening on loudspeakers. After several songs-prayers—King delivered a short but eloquent speech, which many believe began the civil rights movement in earnest:

> *"We're here this evening for serious business. We're here in a general sense because, first and foremost, we are American citizens and we are determined to*

acquire our citizenship to the fullness of its meaning. We are here also because our deep-seated belief that democracy transformed from thin paper to thick action is the greatest form of government on earth.

There comes a time that people get tired. We are here this evening to say to those who have mistreated us so long that we are tired-tired of being segregated and humiliated; tired of being kicked about by the brutal feet of oppression.

There comes a time, my friends, when people get tired of being plunged across the abyss of humiliation, when they experience bleakness of nagging despair. There comes a time when people get tired of being pushed out of the glimmering sunlight of last July and left standing amid the piercing chill of an Alpine November.

We have no alternative ... For many years we have shown amazing patience. We have sometimes given our white brothers the feeling that we liked the way we were being treated. But we come here tonight to be saved from that patience that makes us patient with anything less than freedom and justice."

With those words, the civil rights movement was launched. Now, after 40 years of negotiation, we find ourselves with more blueprints and more plans and a structure that is yet to be completed. For the nineties we have equipped ourselves with new architects and new strategies ...

There is no denying that progress has been made, that we have come a long way, but there are still great distances to be traveled. Change is occurring rapidly. We welcome it. We plan to be a part of it. We want to assist in changing America and, as necessary, in changing ourselves.

First, we envision changing the way we interact with our government. We want to fully participate in political and civic affairs. We recognize that America has other priorities, but we insist that we e one. Minority members of the President's Commission for the Eighties (including Dorothy Height, Benjamin Hooks and Addie Wyatt) recognized over a decade ago the need for us to change even as we change America. They agreed with the commission's emphasis on the need to restore economic growth and stability in

America. They believe, however, that to achieve these goals the nation must adopt and follow policies that promote full employment while providing sufficient public investment necessary to support balanced economic growth...

As African Americans in the nineties, we have rise to new heights and taken on new responsibilities. We are present in city halls, capital rotundas, and for the first time in decades, in both the U.S. House and in the Senate. In increasing numbers, African Americans are assuming the mantle of leadership-from national security adviser to joint chief of staff, from national party chairman to secretary of commerce, and from state health chief to surgeon general... It would be unconscionable to deny us the full privileges of our citizenship; but there is a difference in the opportunity to participate, the privilege of being included, and ultimate success. There is no guarantee of success. Government owes us an opportunity, not a promise. Government owes us a chance, not a prize. In the eighties, we saw a black man in competition for his party's nomination for president. In the nineties, we may well see parties in competition to nominate a black man for president.

Next, if we are to succeed, we must recognize the value of self-sufficiency. The kind of self-sufficiency which removes people from the welfare rolls and the rolls of homelessness, and puts them on the taxpayer rolls. We must help America recognize the nexus between education, job training and self-sufficiency.

The U.S. Conference of Mayors has identified the lack of affordable housing for low-income people as the main cause for homelessness. They have also cited unemployment, mental illness, and domestic violence as contributing causes. We can no longer continue without recognizing, as Kind did years ago, that these problems are linked and that piecemeal solutions will only yield piecemeal results. We need an unwavering commitment to education, job training and health care ...

We know, also, that we have to change the way in which we view ourselves. Renewed pride is, and preservation of, our cultural heritage and traditions is essential. Richard Wright once wrote that three-plus centuries of enslavement destroyed the very images and symbols of our culture and caused our folkways and folk tales to fade from consciousness. We became, by sheer necessity, a secretive people who exalted virtue, revered education, glorified ambition, and celebrated individuality.

And, with animal-like ferocity, we guarded our cherished families. This too has disappeared. Our future depends upon the reestablishment of the family unit, family values, and family stability. Training and parenting skills will go a long way in keeping our children off the streets and out of gangs because the love and acceptance they so badly need will be found in the family. Our cultural heritage is not symbolized by beads and braids but by a deep spiritual commitment, as history resplendent with art, music, literature and dance. Thus, we make take extraordinary pride in its preservation.

Finally, in our contract with America, we must guarantee changes in the ways we address the problems of welfare and homelessness for the less fortunate of our society and the way we address the problems of health care and safety for all Americans. We hear daily the clamor for welfare reforms. Few will deny that the welfare system needs to be reformed-a reformation aimed at eliminating the bureaucratic waste and larceny in welfare agencies, not in removing dependent children and needy recipients from the rolls. The effort to enact a comprehensive health care and health insurance plan has come to a halt but we must be assured that our great society will make affordable health care available to all in the near future...

Among the most vocal elements in our society who are the environmentalists. They are active in protecting life-from the smallest insects to the largest animals-from extinction. But, who will protect our children from extinction by the disease of rat-infested ghettos, the violence of ethnic and territorial gangs armed with the most lethal of weapons, the drug dealers who lure 8-and-10 year-olds into their lucrative trade and exact the same genocide upon them as upon their drug-hardened counterparts? These concerns must be incorporated in any contract we make for a better America.

Finally, it is apparent that a fitting tribute to Dr. King is a rededication of our hearts and minds to the building of a better America. Now is not the time to turn the clock of our progress back, not for one hour or even for one minute. We cannot afford the luxury of an extra hour of sleep, an extra hour of idleness. Every day, every hour, every minute is precious. Use them.

With our commitment, Dr. King's message of yesterday will reverberate today, tomorrow, and tomorrow. His voice will resound as eloquently as ever as we appeal to the nation's conscience to keep his dream alive. Unless we rededicate ourselves and persevere in building a just America, we need not ask "for whom the bell tolls." I fear that it will toll for our shattered dreams.

VIRGIL WOOD

Martin Luther King and Joseph: Discovering, and Setting Free, God's Dream

Dr. Virgil A. Wood and Ryan J. Hulbert, Ph. D.

God's dream for all of His children worldwide remains the same throughout all time. There have been specific individuals, groups, and locations throughout time where that dream has been shared and championed. There have been other times when that dream, has lain dormant in the hearts, minds, and lives of a remnant of people. The purpose of this message is to highlight examples of that dream being set free in the past, and provide an opportunity in the present to be part of a movement to strategically harness the hearts, souls, minds, and strengths, of individuals, resulting in a ripple effect of God's dream to be continually set free, just as King proclaimed "Free at last!"

What is God's Dream?

Bishop Desmond Tutu described God's dream and our possible role in it in this way:

> *... before we can become God's partners, we must know what God wants for us. "I have a dream," God says. "Please help Me to realize it. It is a dream of a world whose ugliness and squalor and poverty, its war and hostility, its greed and harsh competitiveness, its alienation and disharmony are changed into their glorious counterparts, when there will be more laughter, joy, and peace, where there will be justice and goodness and compassion and love and caring and sharing. I have a dream that swords will be beaten into plowshares and spears into pruning hooks, that my children will know they are members of one family, the human family, God's family, My family." (God has a Dream: A vision of hope for our time, 2005, pp.19-20).*

God's dream described above, can be seen in a simplified fashion of the elements of interpersonal harmony, and through the agricultural metaphors of plowshares and pruning hooks, sharing of food and physical prosperity. In other words, His dream can be seen as a vision of **caring** and **sharing**.

A Dreamer in the Distant Past

As an example of an ancient sharer of God's Dream, let us put the spotlight on Joseph, the son of Jacob. We discover through his biography, with all the twists and turns in his life, a pathway for those who desire is to become faithful servants of God's dream. As a youth he had this Dream, which no one understood then, including himself. We learn from his biography that he was sold as a slave by his jealous brothers, brought by slave traders into Egypt, and spent 14 years in an Egyptian prison. However, through divine intervention, inspiration, resisting temptation, and tremendous personal effort, eventually he was a means of bringing much good to his captor nation then in famine, and to his own family, including the brothers who originally sold him into slavery.

One of the most tender scenes in all of the biblical record is Joseph forgiving his brothers, pledging to their abundant future, they together, weeping and reconciling. That reconciling only came about by mighty change of heart, on both Joseph's and his brothers' part. We see here the basic elements of God's dream shown in fixing broken hearts and feeding hungry stomachs, pathway through famine, to the abundance of Beloved Community and Beloved Economy, binary, and undivided.

Even though Joseph's life was filled with tremendous struggles, he later realized that his life was part of God's plan and dream: "And Joseph said to them[his brothers], Fear not: for am I in the place of God? But as for you, you thought evil against me; but God meant it unto good, to bring to pass, as it is this day, *to save much people alive*" (Genesis 50:19-20).

The lives of Joseph and his family were at the beginning of a 400-year period of time in Egypt, with much of that being as slaves in Egypt. Finally, after those 400 years, their then prophet and leader, Moses, led the nation of Israel out of bondage. Although Moses helped his nation come close to the promised land, he was not allowed to enter the Promised Land

The Dream Marches On

Dr. Martin Luther King, Jr. emerged on the Lincoln Memorial Steps, August 28th, 1963 at the historic March on Washington, declaring "I Have

A Dream", culminating a Trek of over 250,000 marchers, from every nook and cranny of the nation.

This speech was shared also near the end of a 400-year period of time in the land that became the nation of the United States of America, and Martin Luther King Jr., emerged as an important National Leader. That nation was founded on the claim "that all people are created equal, and endowed by their Creator with the inalienable right of life, liberty, and the pursuit of happiness, though more in the breach, than the practice.

With those guiding light principles claimed from the very beginning of our nation, the realization of that dream has only gradually unfolded, and is not yet complete.

Clearly, we as a nation, have not yet fulfilled this dream of a promised land. Dr. King stated that he had been able to see this dream fulfilled in the future, because he had "Been to the mountaintop" where the vision of the dream was clearer. Several lines from Dr. King's "I have a dream" speech are quoted below: "I have a dream that one day this nation will rise up and live out the true meaning of its creed: 'We hold these truths to be self-evident: that all men are created equal.' "With this faith we will be able to transform the jangling discords of our nation into a beautiful symphony of brotherhood."

Dr. King highlighted the concept of Beloved Community to describe the symphony of brotherhood and sisterhood. In addition, he spoke of a Beloved Community's Economy, which was necessary to fulfill the elements of God's dream of caring and sharing, of fixing broken hearts and feeding hungry stomachs.

Since Martin's dream was declared over 50 years ago, perhaps our nation has made some progress, but in many ways we have wandered in the wilderness, and not yet reached the promised land of the sacred dream of a beloved America.

The Dream Beckoning

Each of us need to answer for ourselves, in our time, deeply important questions concerning God's dream. In each of our individual lives, with the various twists and turns, we need to ask questions such as, "Am I part of a divinely inspired dream, or am I simply part of an earthly nightmare of strife and disunity?" "Did God mean for my experiences to result in good, to save much people alive?" "Am I helping God in fulfilling His dream of beloved caring communities and beloved sharing economies?"

We invite individuals to help Free the Dream. We believe that this will happen as individuals become part of a movement and take practical steps become a Beloved Citizen Neighbor. We have created a method for people to consider taking a pledge to join this movement and commit themselves to fulfilling the pledge.

The Pledge is the Following:

"I believe that all people, including myself, are of great worth, and are part of the same family of the human race. I pledge to improve myself, and to support people in their physical, educational, economic, and emotional needs. I further

pledge myself to honor the Creator of the world by using one day in a week for devotion and renewal. I believe that these actions will result in overcoming poverty, discovering and raising beloved economic communities, globally, and locally."

We invite you to join us in taking and following the pledge, enhancing our own souls, and thereby healing the soul of America. This movement need not take all of us to make a major difference, but does require some to step forward with love, faith and courage. Famous anthropologist Margaret Mead stated, "Never doubt that a small group of thoughtful, committed citizens can change the world. Indeed, it is the only thing that ever has."

Regardless of what has gone on in the past, each of us in the present have the opportunity to choose for ourselves the pattern we will follow. We choose to follow the pledge, and invite you to do the same.

Future of the Dream

Beginning now, all interested persons can choose to be part of God's dream as the future unfolds. Beginning with each person, the unfolding ripple through families, neighborhoods, and communities, Beloved Citizen

Neighbors can assist in healing the soul of our Nation.

To join this nation-wide movement, please go to the website beloved-communityamerica.com. Then select USA, and then select either English or Spanish. All at no cost, you are invited to follow a 5-minute several step process of taking the pledge, downloading a personalized certificate, and then are given the opportunity of downloading two books designed to help equip you to be an even better Beloved Citizen Neighbor.

Dr. Virgil A. Wood is the author of In Love We Trust: Lessons I learned from Martin Luther King, Jr. and Sr., and was a 10-year working associate of Dr. Martin Luther King, Jr., and 16 additional years with Martin Luther King, Sr.

Ryan J Hulbert, Ph.D. is a licensed psychologist and the author of *The Sun is Always Shining, Drivers' Ed for the Brain, Growth Rings, Are you Settling for Half of the Rainbow?*, and *Which Came First, the Soul or the Ego?*

Afterward:
A Poetic Conclusion

VIRGIL WOOD

Keepers of the world house dream
(Big Momma's Jubilee)

We the keepers
Of the world house dream,
Are all
God's children.

We are old folks with dreams
We are young folks with visions,
We are the sons and daughters Coming from all the nations,
We come testifying
We come prophesying.

We love the Lord
God heard our cry,
And pitied every groan
Long as we live
When troubles rise,
We-the young
And
We the old-
Will hasten to God's throne.

We may be black, or
We may be white,
We may be red,
Brown, yellow,
Or any other color;
But,
Whoever

or
Whatever
We are,
We are all
God's people.
We come from a fat table of big trouble It always comes double,
Racism and poverty
Joblessness and despair,
Fat cats and skinny nations
War and armament sales,
Drugs and alcohol
Homelessness and greed,
All these our troubles,
They keep on being doubles!
When will it ever end?

Thank God, Momma also got a table
An international order,
Of the world house dream.

The table Big Momma set,
Is round like the world,
Is open like God's arms,
Is plenteous like God's mercy,
Is workable like God's righteousness, Is impartial like God's justice,
Is available like God's faithfulness, Is delicious like God's goodness,
Is friendly like God's kindness,
Is wonderful like God's joy,
And surely
Is harmonious like God's peace,
Truly God's Spirit,

VIRGIL WOOD

In all nine flavors!
Big Momma's table is linked-up;
Connected to the beloved economy,
Assembled for the world house Made in America,
Truly, our best export.

This big, fat, round table
Set
By Godly people,
By Mays, by Mary, and by Martin; By all ofus who chose to be,
In service, as living associates.
Come, my Beloved
My Sisters and My Brothers
Of the whole wide world,
Earth's bounty is God's blessing,
Earth's goodness, is our total birthright;
Earth shall have her jubilee. It can't forever
Be denied!

And so my Beloved
Come, let us make bread together on our feet:
Come, let us break bread together,
On our knees ...

... The world house dream,
God's nation of nations,
One blood, many nations, "the 'One-Blood' nation."
Amen ... Shalom ... Asalam alakum ... and Amen!

Tribute to a Dear Spiritual Partner

Go down death, and bring me, Macy - the courageous one!

The other day, on July Fourth, God looked down from Heaven,
And dispatched the mighty Angel Gabriel on a major mission.

God Said, go down death, and fetch me
The courageous, proud, and compassionate soul of Macy.
She has borne her burden, in the heat of the day.
She has suffered long enough. Her work is truly done.
What a mighty work, she has wrought. I now have new work for her
And, for it, she is already well prepared

At a much earlier time, long before her final entry into Eternity,
She gave me her heart, and we stayed in communication through her Soul

She transformed her own mind through my son, Jesus her Christ,
And, by the Holy Spirit, she gave her bodily strength in spite of
serious illness.

To our New Kingdom of Love, and then became; one of its very
Exemplars
When she made her conscious decision and kept it all the way,
A choice of Word over chaos, Life over death, Light over darkness,
and
Love over fear, she cut a streak through the universe.
For any others who choose to, they can now follow, also because of
her light
Yes, She was so faithful in her soul journey, and thus also helped so
many others.
And now she is up here with US, giving Heaven her unique soul

touch, where she has traded Earthly place for Heavenly space. In the process, she helped other humans down there learn how THEY can all, BECOME HUMAN TOGETHER. Her HEADS UP HARTFORD, really got my attention. When she said HEADS UP HARTFORD, she was energizing not only one Metropolis, but her vibes were synergizing nations, and my Whole UNIVERSE.
She has assisted me in transposing HEAVENLY LOVE, making it more natural and present on EARTH.

Surely, you can now understand why, when Angel Gabriel came back from my assignment, searching the whole Earth, and finding one of it's most courageous and compassionate souls,
He blew his horn, with joyful coolness, and wildly with exuberance, and then shouted

HEADS UP, HEAVEN... MACY IS HERE!!!

Macy Reid, whose life of love and courage, will continue to inspire and instruct all ofus who were privileged to share her journey, a partner in Christ, whose place is irreplaceable in this work we shared, went home to be with God, July 4, 2006.

C.I.R.C.U.L.E.O*

When love Circulates - throughout communities

THE CIRCULATION OF LOVE
LIKE THE FLOW OF THE BLOOD
IS ABSOLUTELY ESSENTIAL
TO THE HEALTH OF THE BODY.
AT ANOTHER LEVEL, THE CIRCULATION OF THE MONEY
TO ALL PARTS OF THE BODY POLITIC
IS ESSENTIAL
TO THE HEALTH AND VITALITY OF THE WHOLE BODY
ECONOMIC.

THE WHOLE BODY NEEDS LOVE,
AS WELL AS MONEY, AS WELL AS BLOOD.
GOOD CIRCULATION ENSURES GOOD HEALTH. HEALTH
IS MEASURED BY VITALITY AND VIABILITY, CIVILITY AND
NOBILITY—
THROUGH THE INVISIBILITY, TRANSPARANCY,
AND INVINCIBILITY OF LOVE.

IF THE BLOOD STOPS FLOWING TO ANY PART OF THE
BODY
THEN THAT PART OF THE BODY WILL DIE SOONER THAN
THE REST.

WHEN THE FLOW OF LOVE IS INTERRUPTED, DIS-EASE
FOLLOWS
WHEN THE FLOW,- OF BLOOD, LOVE, AND MONEY-
—OR COMPASSION, KINDNESS AND JOY, ARE RESUMED—

LIFE AND HEAL TH ALSO COME BACK.

IF SOCIETY WANTS HEALING FROM ANY DISEASE
THEN IT MUST ATTEND TO ALL THOSE FACTORS NECES-
SARY AND SUFFICIENT TO RESTORING HEALTH,
AND TO BRINGING BACK CIVILITY IN CULTURE AND
SOCIETY

IT IS MORE SIMPLE THAN OUR MINDS WILL ADMIT,
LIKE **A COLD DRINK OF WATER**,
GIVEN, APPRECIATED, RECEIVED AND PASSED ON,
'A LITTLE DAB' (OFL.O.V.E.) 'WILL DO YA'.
A LITTLE BIT OF LOVE FROM A WHOLE LOT OF US, IS
ALL IT TAKES,
TO HEAL AND ENJOY, OURSELVES AND OUR FAMILIES,
OUR CULTURE AND OUR WORLD!, TRULY A NEW
COMMUNITY OF LOVE, CAN SAVE OURSELVES UNHAPPINESS
AND THE WORLD ITS MISERY.
YES, A BELOVED COMMUNITY AND ITS ECONOMY!!!

*COMMUNITIES IN RECOVERY, COMMUNICATING,
UNIFYING, AND LOVING EACH OTHER
(Another twelve-step recovery model for communities, Churches, Families
and other institutions)

HOW A LITTLE BIT OF LOVE FROM A WHOLE LOT OF US,
SAVES OURSELVES UNHAPPINESS AND THE WORLD
ITS MISERY!

About the Author

Dr. Virgil A Wood, church leader, educator, and civil rights activist, has committed much of his life's wmk to the struggle for economic and spiritual development among the nation's disadvantaged.

Educated at Virginia Union University and Andover Newton Theological Schooi he holds a doctorate from the Harvard University Graduate School of Education.

Ordained as a Baptist minister in his late teens, Wood has served churches in Rhode Island, Massachusetts, and Virginia. During his pastorate in Lynchburg, Virginia, he became actively involved in the civil rights movement, and served with Martin Luther King, Jr., as member of the National Executive Board of the Southern Christian Leadership Conference, and coordinated the state of Virginia for the historic march to Washington, on April 28, 1963.

Among Wood's publications is the *Introduction to Black Church Economic Studies* (Raleigh, NC: Sparks Press, 1974). Wood was also the originator and contributor of *The Jubilee Bible*, (New York: American Bible Society, 1998).

Wood has combined his dual career in church leadership and education with a lifelong commitment to community development, as economic and spiritual transformation. Dr. Wood is currently the pastor emeritus of the Pond Street Baptist Church, which he has served from 1983 to 2005 (and also from 1955 to 1958). He previously served in higher education as administrator and teacher. Since 2017 he has been Ridenour Faculty Fellow, Virginia Polytechnic Institute, Virginia Tech, leading in developing the Beloved Community Initiative, on the website belovedcommunityinitiative.com.

He is joyfully married to the former Lillian Walker, with whom he shared the joys of parenting their now-grown children; they are also proud grandparents. Dr. and Mrs. Wood live in Houston, Texas. They can be reached by email at drwood@soulscope.com.

Photographs

To my Friend and Co-Worker Virgil Wood In appreciation for your significant ministry and your unswerving devotion to the ideals of freedom and justice

Martin

MLK's Autograph to Wood, Summer 1963

MLK with Children

Abernathy, King & Wood in Conference (April 23, 1965)

Preparation for Historic April 23, 1965 March to Boston Common

Masses March Through the Streets of Boston

Dr. King addressing the 1965 Boston Common Marchers

Abernathy and King (Greeting
long-time Boston friend)

MLK Leading March of 40,000 to
Boston Common (April 23, 1965)

MLK Leading March of 40,000 to Boston Common (April 23, 1965)

Masses March Through the Streets of Boston

Dr. King and Rev. Abernathy (long-time Boston friend)

Boston Turnout to Greet King in 1967 (Poor People's Campaign)

Behind King and Abernathy, stands Deborah (9) and David (8) Wood

King addresses community on steps of Patrick Campbell
School, later named after King

MLK Giving an Autograph to Boston Marcher

MLK, Virgil Wood, & Boston Mayor John F. Collins (1965)

MLK, Wood, and MA Govenor, John Volpe (1965)

MLK, Virgil Wood, & Boston Mayor John F. Collins (1965)

MLK, Wood, and MA Govenor, John Volpe (1965)

MLK, Ralph Abernathy, and Rabbi Abraham Heschel
(Selma to Montgomery March)

Wood, Kivie Kaplan, Rabbie Roland Gittleson,
Ralph Abernathy, Rabbi Harvey Fields, MLK (April 22, 1965)

Virgil and Lillian Wood on their 50th Anniversary

Lillian Wood Making Presentation to Rosa Parks
at the 1989, Hampton Minister's Conference

Virgil Alongside Rosa Parks, who is receiving an Honorary Doctorate

MLK and Wood, Pointing to a Future Victory (April 23, 1965)

The King Legacy to be continued by each of us.

Index

H

Haley, Alex 67, 76, 77, 80
Hamer, Fannie Lou 31
Haughey, John 201, 206
Height, Dr. Dorothy 31
Hudson, Russ 10, 162

J

Jail Trail 6, 8, 42, 84, 86, 88, 90, 91, 92, 95
Jesus Christ 12, 24, 100, 113, 127, 134, 135, 136, 139, 146, 161, 167, 169, 172, 174,
        181-184, 188, 189, 191, 192, 193, 199, 200, 201, 202, 203, 204, 205, 206, 207,
Jones, Mac Charles 32
Jubilee 4, 5, 6, 7, 8, 42, 51, 83, 84, 160, 161, 162, 165, 166, 167, 168, 169, 170, 204,
        205, 208, 209, 222, 229

K

Kelso, Louis D 10, 13, 123, 125, 142, 145, 146
King, Martin Luther, Jr. 4–6, 8, 10, 13,16-18, 21, 22, 23, 26, 27, 29, 30, 57, 65, 67,
        91–97, 99, 100, 101, 103, 104–119, 122–127, 130, 132–141, 145, 146, 155, 157,
        159–162, 165, 166, 175, 209-219, 219–222, 226, 229
King, Martin Luther, Sr. 10, 99
King David 13

L

Ledbetter, Beverly E. 210
Lewis, John 99
Lincoln, Abraham 18, 116, 135
Little, Reverend Earl 71, 72
Lord 149, 154, 166, 167
Lott, Trent 98, 99

M

Mandela, Nelson 91
Mitchell, David 14
Mays, Benjamin Elijah 29, 103, 114, 172, 224
Muhammad, Elijah 68, 78, 80, 81